D0923243

IN OLDE NEW YORK

THE CLIPPER SHIP "DREADNOUGHT"

Capt. S. Samuels, as she appeared February 25, 1854, off Sandy Hook, 19 days from Liverpool. Her record trip was 13 days 11 hours between New York and Liverpool, December 1854. Built at Newburyport, Mass., 1853. Reproduced from an old colored lithographic print.

IN OLDE NEW YORK

SKETCHES OF OLD TIMES AND PLACES IN BOTH THE STATE AND THE CITY

BY

CHARLES BURR TODD

Author of "In Olde Connecticut," "In Olde Massachusetts,"
"The Story of the City of New York," "The
True Aaron Burr," etc.

IRA J. FRIEDMAN, INC.

Port Washington, Long Island, N.Y.

IN OLDE NEW YORK

Published in 1907
Reissued in 1968 by Ira J. Friedman, Inc.
Library of Congress Catalog Card No: 68-18359
Manufactured in the United States of America

EMPIRE STATE HISTORICAL PUBLICATIONS SERIES No. 49

FOREWORD

THIS book is dedicated to the citizens of New York who love her history and traditions. Many of its stories were written twenty years ago and are repeated now with very little change simply because they described types and conditions (especially in the great city) that no longer exist. The generation that read them in 1885 in the *Evening Post* or *Lippincott's Magazine* will re-peruse them as one reads the faces of old friends long forgotten. To the generation which has come on the stage since they were written they will have the novelty and interest of original tales. My publishers and some of my critics have suggested that I adapt them to changed conditions. I let them stand as written.

C. B. T.

OCTOBER, 1907.

CONTENTS

ILLUSTRATIONS

IN OLDE NEW YORK

IN OLDE NEW YORK

CHAPTER I

THE OLD CITY DOCK[1]

A N old time friend of mine, a gentleman of leisure, whenever an attack of ennui threatens, flees to the city docks, where he finds in their bustle and infinite variety an unfailing specific. He stops to inspect whole fleets of canal boats snugly housed during winter from the terrors of the "raging canawl," is thrilled at sight of an ocean steamer just in from a perilous voyage, storm-battered, with torn sails, and decks and rigging sheathed with ice. The great railway docks hold him a long time. On the Southern steamship wharves he draws odorous breaths of resin and tar, trails his cane through little puddles of molasses, and gets his hair full of cotton lint, whereat the stevedores grin. The dock where the trim little fruit schooners from the West Indies unload is a favorite haunt and so are the piers along South Street, below Roosevelt, where the few battered veterans of the California and Canton trade still discharge their cargoes. When his circuit is completed he has studied every

[1] Written in 1883.

nationality, learned the cut of every civilized jib,
heard the music of every tongue, and inspected the
products of the known earth.

The region between the present Coenties Slip and
Whitehall Street my friend finds most prolific of fancies. It is the site of the old city dock, the first built
on Manhattan. This dock was the corner-stone of
the commerce of our metropolis, the progenitor of our
thirty miles or more of wharves. That famous mo-
nopoly, the West India Company, built it, and its
quaint, round-bottomed, high-pooped Dutch ships were
the first vessels here. They gathered the grain, pelts,
lumber, potash, and medicinal herbs that then formed
New Netherland's exports, or landed the hardware,
groceries, household goods, brick, "cow calves" and
"ewe milk sheep," and other peculiar Dutch imports.
As late as 1702 this dock formed almost the sole wharf-
age of the city, and seventy-four vessels, pinks, galleys,
snows, a few brigs and ships, were moored to it during
the year, two thirds of them from the West Indies and
Southern provinces. The town then contained 5250
inhabitants, living in 750 dwellings, so that the wharf
was ample for its needs. As much of the interest and
romance of the old dock gathers about this period
from 1690 to 1700, I may indicate its primitiveness
by the fact that the city streets were first lighted in
1697, by hanging a lantern on a pole before every
seventh house "in the dark time of the moon," and

that the city police force consisted of four honest
citizens whose office was to walk the streets at night
sounding a bell and proclaiming the hour and state of
the weather.

Along the rude dock at that time we should have
seen, here a galley from Fayal, there a " pink " from
Barbadoes, in its neighbor a "snow" from Boston or
the Virginias, with possibly a full-rigged bark or ship
from London unloading cargo, for England was as
determined then as later that her American colonies
should receive their European products through her
own bottoms and warehouses. It is likely, too, that
a trim, buoyant vessel, painted black, with long taper-
ing masts and spars, would be lying at the wharf —
a slave trader lately in from the coast of Guinea, and
about to sail for a new cargo. As soon as the stout
burghers of Manhattan acquired a little wealth in
stock and lands they felt the need of servants, and
despatched ships to the coast of Africa after them.
Strange adventures and many dangers attended these
early traders; if they escaped the pirates which then
swarmed in all frequented seas, they ran into some little
port along the Angola coast, bargained with the petty
king of the place for a contingent, and so creeping
along the shore made up their cargo from a score of
villages, provided, however, that some piratical craft
did not follow them into harbor and capture craft,
cargo and all. For these were the days of such free-

booting in the colonies as seems incredible to modern ears.

In our character of dreamer we shall see a dim, shadowy vessel far out in the offing that does not come boldly up to the wharf like an honest craft, but tacks and fills as if waiting an assurance that the coast is clear before venturing in. While we are speculating about her a long boat appears coming from her direction, in whose bow stands a stout, swarthy, bearded man, his sinister face tanned by Indian suns, a fine, beautifully wrought gold chain from Arabian workshops about his neck, rings set with gems on his fingers, and under his coat a netted belt through whose meshes we catch the gleam of gold. Once ashore he makes his way to the Governor's mansion, whence he presently returns smiling and rubbing his hands gleefully, and then hurries away to the ship. Next morning we gather with the crowd to see the latter berthed, and when this is done and the hatches removed, bale after bale of costly merchandise is hauled up and carried away. One might fancy himself for the nonce transported to the Orient. Tea and cassia, rich silks of China, woven fabrics of Cashmere, Indian sandal wood, perfumes, and gems, spices and gums of Ceylon. African gold and ivory, with half the products of European workshops, the vessel pours out, until half-a-million dollars in value has passed from her hold. There is no doubt as to the character of the craft; she

THE OLD CITY DOCK

As it appeared in 1746. Reproduced from an old wood-cut

belonged to that powerful guild of pirates which at this period, under the corrupt Governor Fletcher, had become one of the wealthiest interests of the city.

These colonial pirates at this distance of time seem the ideal freebooters. As a rule they were the most enterprising shipmasters of their day, who were drawn from the merchant service into privateering during the French and Spanish wars, and on the return of peace, impatient of restraint, became privateers on general principles and turned their guns on vessels of every flag. The whole waste of waters was their cruising ground, but their special field was the Indian Ocean. With characteristic ingenuity they reduced the business to a system. The home merchants, who in many cases had fitted them out and had a share in the profits, established lines of swift vessels to Madagascar, the rendezvous of the pirates, which carried out such supplies as they might need and brought back the booty to be disposed of as lawful merchandise, the pirates themselves returning home only at intervals. What seductive pictures must have been painted for the adventurous youth of Gotham in 1690-6 when the pirate captains were beating up the town for recruits! Fighting and bloodshed were not mentioned; the prizes were unarmed and would yield to a show of strength. And in sober truth these calculations were correct. East India piracy was not a bloody trade; captured crews and passengers were in most cases well

treated and put ashore at the nearest point. At the
trial of Captain Kidd his prosecutors could not fix a
single murder upon him, except that of a mutinous
member of his crew. With such inducements scores
of vessels fitted out from the colonial ports, chiefly
from New York and Rhode Island. Had they been
content with plundering the Dutch and native traders,
they might have continued to flourish for years; but
when, grown bolder, they began taking the rich bottoms
of the East India Company, that powerful corporation
began taking steps to suppress them.

The era of the California and Canton clipper ships
was one of which America may justly be proud, and,
singularly enough, the trade which they created centered in the neighborhood, if not on the site, of the old
city dock.

They had their origin in the advantages which our
shrewd merchants of 1845 saw lay in quick passages
to the East, but they were brought to perfection by
the California gold mining excitement of '49 and succeeding years. During their existence, they gave us
the supremacy of the seas, excited the keenest rivalry
between American and English ship-builders, and became the theme of international comment. Yet one
looks in vain for any account of them in the published
histories of the city, while the opening of the Pacific
Railway and the development of steam navigation
so revolutionized the machinery of commerce that

merchants of to-day have almost forgotten their existence.   The two lines of clippers were of nearly simultaneous origin, the one in part the complement of the other.

In the winter of 1848–9 New York wore an air of suppressed excitement: in counting-room and office, tavern and exchange, there was one common topic of conversation — gold; until, at length, the spell of it fell on half the energetic men of the city.   The spring before, a workman clearing out a mill-race on a branch of the Sacramento had found particles of gold.   The discovery leaked out despite the efforts made to keep it secret; it floated over the mountains, came around the Horn, and brought unrest and disquiet not only to the Atlantic seaboard cities, but to the old world centers of capital and population as well.   Many yet remember the scenes of bustle and excitement produced by the news.   Ordinary methods of money-making seemed slow or superannuated compared with the picking up of gold nuggets in the river beds.   The newspapers fanned the flame by publishing interviews with returned Californians, and every scrap of news concerning the diggings that could be gathered.   The *Herald* published California specials, and tales of twenty-five and twenty-eight pound nuggets picked up by lucky miners.   Associations were at once formed for proceeding to the gold regions.   Clothing men turned their attention to providing mining outfits;

patent medicine men evolved specifics against chills, fevers, rheumatisms, and other diseases incident to a new country; publishers advertised "choice reading, suitable for voyagers to the Pacific," and inventors placed in the field a bewildering and ludicrous array of contrivances for camping and gold-washing. Patent mess hampers, folding tables, and dressing cases, gold detecting scales, portable India rubber beds that could quickly be inflated for use, and houses of the same material that could be put up or taken down in a few hours, figure in the advertisements of the day. "I first heard the news, I think, in February, 1849," said an old pioneer, "from the wife of Clerk Gallagher, of Washington Market. She had a babe barely a month old, and was in a pretty condition at her husband's leaving her and going to the mines. As we were talking Gallagher came in, and I remarked that I felt like laying my stick across his back for his cruelty in leaving wife and baby. 'Ah,' said he, 'wait till you hear it all,' and he sat down and told me such tales of the mines that when he had finished I was ready to leave my desk and family and set out for the diggings. There was witchcraft in it, you see."

The first pioneers went around Cape Horn, usually chartering their vessel and furnishing their own outfits. The later and more favorite route was across Mexico, and later still over the Isthmus. The first to lead a party over the Mexican route was Col. J. C.

Battersby, of New York City, favorably known during the war as commander of the First New York Lincoln Cavalry, and for his war sketches in *Harper's Weekly*. The Colonel's reminiscences of the event are entertaining. "It was in March, 1849," he says, "that I hired a room at No. 2 Dey Street and advertised to lead a company of men across Mexico to California in sixty days at $250 each. It was the first time, to my knowledge, that the idea had been broached. The usual method for gold-diggers then was to form an association of perhaps fifty or a hundred members, charter a vessel, procure outfits, and sail around the Cape, a voyage of five or six months. As showing that there were those incredulous as to the richness of the new Eldorado, I may mention that soon after my advertisement appeared, the owner of the building came to me and said he would have no more men roped in there and their money taken away. 'You tell them,' said he, 'there's gold in California, and I don't believe there's that gold in California,' indicating a section of his thumb nail as large as a pea. 'Very well,' said I, and secured rooms of Richard French, on or near the spot where the Belmont Hotel now stands.

"The plan was so novel, however, and untried, that few presented themselves. I secured but one, Dr. N. S. Murphy, an Irish physician of character and attainments. I had chartered the bark *Eugenia*,

owned by Peter Argus & Co., and, after holding her
three weeks for the desired number, put my horse, my
Newfoundland dog, Rubens, and my outfit on board,
and embarked with the doctor for Vera Cruz where
we arrived in thirty-one days.   From that port we took
the National Road to the City of Mexico twelve days,
thence by easy stages through the valley of Guarrnica,
later Maximilian's summer retreat, to Acapulco.
Here the doctor was taken ill with burning fever and
lay forty days in the Governor's palace, where we were
hospitably entertained.   Just as he was well enough
to travel, the British steamer *Unicorn* came into port
eight months from New York with 600 passengers on
board bound for San Francisco.   Cabins, decks, fore-
castle, everything was full, except the upper compart-
ment of a large coop on the main deck which had been
used for the storage of fowls: this we secured for $100
each, and in this queer cabin made the voyage to San
Francisco."

The vast influx of gold-seekers into California
naturally induced a demand for all sorts of goods, and
to supply these and at the same time furnish quick
passenger service, the merchants of New York and
Boston provided the clipper lines. J. & N. Briggs,
40 South Street; E. B. Sutton, 119 Wall; James Smith,
116 Wall; E. Richards & Co., 52 South; Thomas
Wardle, 88 South; E. W. Kimball & Co., 84 Wall;
C. H. & W. Pierson, 61 South; and N. L. McCready

& Co., 36 South, figure in the advertisements of the day as the principal ship owners in the California trade, all of them, it will be noticed, in the vicinity of the old city dock. This section of the water front never had seen, and never will see again, such scenes of bustle and animation as then enlivened it. Truck after truck loaded with lumber, groceries, provisions, clothing, mining implements, and miners' outfits crowded it from morning till night. Groups of pioneers roughly clad in suits of tough, ill-smelling, English cloth, with pockets covering all available space, wives and children bidding them tearful farewells, the departure of half-a-dozen vessels a day, were the scenes there presented.

The trade with California was a very unsatisfactory one for the merchants engaged, owing to the fluctuating character of the market. Many fortunes were lost as well as made in the business, and many cargoes shipped that did not pay the charges, the ship owners being often obliged to sue for their freight money. An instance of this uncertainty was narrated by Colonel Battersby. On arriving at San Francisco he had written a letter to a friend in New York, cashier of the Chemical Bank, in which he mentioned casually the abundance and cheapness of provisions in the city. As the cashier was reading it a gentleman came in to draw out $50,000, remarking as he did so that he was about sending a cargo of provisions to California, as

they were all starving out there. On hearing the
Colonel's letter, however, he decided to relinquish the
venture.   Perhaps it was this uncertainty of a market,
perhaps the competition of the steamers, that led the
more enterprising merchants to make San Francisco
only a port of call, and to send their clipper ships over
the Pacific to the rich ports of China and India; at
least about this time originated the Canton tea trade
as a distinctive business of the port.

Of course, there had been trade with China before,
but the California clippers were not in it. Salem,
fifty years earlier, had boldly announced herself a
competitor with Europe for the trade of the Orient,
and had demonstrated the superiority of small, swift
vessels in the transportation of teas and rich cargoes.
Boston and New York now began to put in commission
those magnificent clippers that for speed and seafaring
qualities have never been equaled, and which, but
for the development of the steam marine, would certainly have wrested from England her boasted supremacy of the seas. Most of the shrewd, far-seeing
merchants and skilled sea captains who carried on this
enterprise have done with ledger and log-book, and
sleep in Greenwood or in the coral depths. A single
firm the writer succeeded in finding in Burling Slip,
and was kindly allowed to mouse among its scrap-
books and records at will.

The great object aimed at in these clippers was

speed, and their owners had the English as well as the American market in mind in their construction. If the English merchant could secure his cargo of tea or silks from Canton in an American bottom a month earlier than in an English one, they argued, interest would prompt him to charter the quicker craft. It was found, too, the longer a cargo of tea was on the water the more it deteriorated. "Speed" was therefore the order given the American ship-builder. The more famous clipper ship-yards were those of W. H. Webb and Jacob Westervelt in Brooklyn, Charles Mallory and Greenwood & Sons, Mystic, Ct., and Donald McKay, East Boston. The clippers were sharp, comparatively narrow for their length, and models of trimness and grace. Some were of large tonnage, the *Eternal* for instance registered 1800 tons, the *Staghound* 1534, the *Sovereign of the Seas*, built by Donald McKay, 2421. Later the *Young America*, of New York, was turned out, registering eighty tons more, whereupon Mr. McKay expressed his determination to build a ship of 3500 tons to carry 4000 tons of merchandise to California. As a rule, however, the true Canton clippers were vessels of from 500 to 1000 tons burden. Some of the quick passages they made approached the incredible, and exceeded the quickest steamer time of the day. In 1852 there were in commission the clipper ships *Surprise, Celestial, Sea Witch, Samuel Russell, Staghound, George E.*

Webster, and barks *Race Horse* and *Memnon*, all of which had made the passage from New York to San Francisco in from ninety to one hundred and twenty days, the average steamer time being one hundred and fifty. The clipper ship *Northern Light* once sailed from San Francisco to Boston in seventy-six days, five hours; and in a trial of speed with the *Contest* in 1853 made the passage to New York in seventy-three days. The log-book of the ship *Samuel Russell*, one of New York's finest vessels, in a voyage from China home, showed a total of 6722 miles run in thirty days, the greatest distance in one day being 318, or $13\frac{1}{4}$ miles per hour. The same ship sailed from Whampoa, China, February 5, 1848, passed Angiers on the 15th, Cape of Good Hope March 18, the equator April 6, and took the New York pilot April 27.

One gets no idea of the *esprit* and dash of the clippers, however, unless he stumbles on some idle tar of the many on South Street, who formerly served in the fleet. Mention a Canton clipper to such a one, and his eyes glisten, and his tongue wags fast. "There was nothin' like 'em for prettiness," he observes, "and the way they jist did flog all other craft out of the water. I remember once we was at Hong Kong in the *Sam'l Russell*, and as there was a Britisher leaving for New York, we sent home letters by him. 'Bout a month later the *Russell* cleared on the same tack, an' she did drive on that voyage like a race horse.

Sail after sail she overhauled and left behind: roundin
the Cape, I remember, the Jack Tars started the
sayin' that 'the old man couldn't hold his horses in.'
But flyin' up the coast of Brazil what did we do but
skip by that Britisher that had our letters on board
and make port a week ahead of him, delivering 'em
by word of mouth. Another voyage I was on that
racer, the *Flyin' Cloud*, comin' home from Hong
Kong. I tell you 'twas as bracin' as a glass of grog
to stand on her top hamper and feel her pull, comin'
down the trades. Once in a while a brother Yankee
would give us a tug before we could shake him off,
but as for anythin' foreign, English, Dutch, or French,
we handled 'em as though they was babies. There
was one thing the ship did on that v'yage that I've allus
blamed her owners or nearest relations fer not spin'in'
a yarn on. One day we took a pretty smart breeze
on the starboard quarter, and held it tolerably steady
for the space of ten days, in which time, sir, we made
upwards of forty-five degrees, hard on to 3200 miles,
328 miles one day, as the log will show. Ther's
another thing; bein' so long and narrer, you'd expect
the clippers would ship some water, but all that v'yage,
I didn't see a gallon o' water on the ship's deck, not
enough to wash her down with."

American ships continued to rule the wave, until
superseded by the more reliable steamers. But what
a turn in fortune's wheel! In 1853 American ships

securing cargoes in English home ports amid the fiercest competition; in 1883 almost every pound of America's exports afloat in British bottoms, and scarcely an American vessel in commission in the foreign trade!

CHAPTER II

IN 1880, St. Patrick's churchyard was one of the few in the densely populated portion of the city remaining intact, and had long been closed to interments except by special permit of the Board of Health.

A blank brick wall hid it from the three streets Mulberry, Mott, and Prince that bounded it: the old Cathedral of St. Patrick overshadowed it, while the office of the Calvary Cemetery Association formed part of the northern boundary.

If one hunted up the old sexton and was admitted he found little turf within, little shade, a litter of twigs and leaves on the ground, some of the tombstones shattered, and others overthrown or leaning far out of the perpendicular; while the voices of the few birds that harbored there were drowned by the discordant noises of a squalid neighborhood.

In this ground a tombstone was long ago erected with this inscription:

A La Memoire
de
Pierre de Landais,
Ancien Contre Admiral
au service
Des Etats Unis.
Qui disparut
June, 1818,
ae 87 ans.

For forty years prior to the above date Pierre Landais had been one of the noted characters of the city. He claimed the rank of "Admiral," and those who would retain his favor were obliged to observe a punctilious regard for the title. His short, stout figure clad in a faded Continental uniform — cocked hat, small sword, knee breeches, and all — seated in the shade of Printing-House Square or pacing slowly down Broadway to the Bowling Green — his favorite promenade — was a familiar object to the New Yorkers of one hundred years ago. In the coffee-houses and inns, equal sharers of his attentions, he never failed of a circle of admirers to whom he recounted stirring tales of sea fights in which he had been an actor, and generally concluded with an account of his capture of the *Serapis* and *Countess of Scarborough*, and a hearty denunciation of the man who had stolen the laurels of that conflict from him. His persistency as a claimant

ST. PATRICK'S CEMETERY

In the centre of the foreground is the tombstone of Admiral de Landais. From a photograph taken in 1907, especially for "In Olde New York"

before Congress alone made him noteworthy. He
had claims for arrears of pay and for prize money,
and urged them for forty years until he became the
Nestor of American claimants. Every year, at the
sitting of Congress, he hurried to Washington in the
lumbering old coaches that then connected the cities,
and haunted the lobbies and galleries of the Capitol
like an unquiet spirit, deluging Congress with petitions
and memorials, watching its proceedings with feverish
interest, and button-holing members at every opportunity in the interest of his claims. In the journals
of Congress no name appears more frequently among
the petitioners and memorialists than his; but although
his petitions were personally urged, and often accompanied by letters offering cogent reasons why his claims
should be allowed, they were never granted, and the
old man, year by year, returned to his lodgings at
the close of the session as empty as he went, to renew
the conflict with poverty, and live in the hope of
better fortune another year.

His history has the elements of a romance. One
cannot but feel, too, on reviewing his career, that there
may have been a grain of injustice in the treatment he
received from his adopted country. He was born a
Count of France, and early rose to the command of a
French line-of-battle ship, but relinquished all in
1777 to join his fortunes with those of the young republic across the sea, then engaged in her gallant

stand for liberty. Baron Steuben recommended him, and Silas Deane, then American Commissioner to France, gave him the command of the ship *Heureux*, rechristened the *Flammand*, recently purchased to convey military stores to America. His commission, dated March 1, 1777, was accompanied by this interesting letter from the worthy Commissioner: "I give you a commission to use in case of necessity or advantage in making a prize, but you are not to go out of your course for that purpose. You will keep an account of your expenses, which will be paid you on your arrival in America. I shall write to the Congress by other conveyances, and assure them that you have received nothing but your expenses, and your generous confidence in them will not pass unnoticed." So good an authority as the Marine Committee of Congress testified to the skill and address with which Landais executed this commission, in eluding the British cruisers sent to intercept him, and bringing the *Flammand* safely into port. Congress also showed its appreciation of him by commissioning him a captain in the navy, and ordered 12,000 livres to be paid him "as a pecuniary consideration equal to his services." The Marine Committee also gave him the oversight of the ships-of-war then building at Portsmouth and Salisbury for the newly-created navy, in their report to Congress styling him "an excellent sea officer, and skilled in the construction of ships-of-war." The next

summer he enjoyed a still more signal mark of its
favor. On the 29th of May, 1778, the *Alliance*, a fine
and uncommonly fast frigate of thirty-six guns, was
launched at Salisbury, Mass., where she had been long
building. She went into commission June 19, and for
her maiden voyage was ordered to transport the Mar-
quis de Lafayette and suite to France. Her commander, duly commissioned by Congress, was the
Admiral Pierre Landais. The memorable voyage of
the *Alliance*, the motley character of her crew — a
part of whom were English seamen from a vessel
wrecked on the Massachusetts coast — how these
mutinied as the vessel neared the British coast, and
how the mutiny was promptly quelled by Landais,
and the vessel safely brought into Brest, is told in
history.

In France Landais met his evil genius in the person
of the famous Admiral John Paul Jones. Landais
had his faults, being haughty, imperious, punctilious,
quarrelsome, and a martinet. Jones was all this and
more, and the two were at enmity from the moment
of meeting. They met first in August, 1779, at Brest,
where a little squadron composed of four French
vessels and the *Alliance* had rendezvoused in order to
make a swoop on the Baltic fleet then about due in
England. Jones, in command of the *Bon Homme
Richard*, was the senior officer, and there was trouble
before the fleet sailed as to who should command it,

but the matter was amicably settled at last by each
of the five commanders signing an agreement to act
in concert under the commissions received from Congress. The squadron got under way August 14, and
on the 23d of September met the Baltic fleet, con-
voyed by the *Serapis* and *Countess of Scarborough*.
The details of the engagement that followed are so
familiar that I need not repeat them. The charges
so frequently made against Captain Landais by Jones
in his report of the affair to Franklin, and corroborated
by the statements of other officers of the fleet, merit
attention. It was charged that the *Alliance* held aloof
at the opening of the engagement, and that when she
came to the aid of the *Bon Homme Richard*, then
engaged with the *Serapis*, she poured her broadsides
into the former, and repeated the maneuver again
and again, never once striking the *Serapis* except
over or through the decks of the *Richard*. The report
did more than this — it distinctly charged the commander of the *Alliance*, first with cowardice and then
with treachery — that he designed to sink the *Richard*
in order to win for himself the glory of capturing the
Serapis. These charges were generally accepted as
true by the American public of that day, and have
passed into history as truth. This paper makes no
attempt to disprove them. It is but due to Captain
Landais to say, however, that he met them with an
indignant denial, and that he at once demanded a

trial, where he might be confronted with his accusers, which demand was not granted.

He showed himself to be no craven, however, by calling out one of his defamers — Captain Cottineau, of the *Pallas* — and running him through with his smallsword. This exploit he followed up by challenging the commander of the *Bon Homme Richard*. No meeting, however, took place. Franklin, obliged to notice the charges, ordered Landais to Paris to answer them; but although the latter promptly presented himself at the capital, and used every effort to that effect, he failed to secure a trial.

Finding his efforts there fruitless, Landais, early in 1780, applied to Franklin for leave to go to America to answer the charges preferred against him there. Franklin, no doubt glad to have the affair off his hands, consented, and ordered his expenses paid. A few weeks later, March 17, Landais wrote again to Franklin asking to be reinstated in command of the *Alliance*, which had by this time come into French waters and was lying at L'Orient, and which, it was rumored, was soon to sail with stores for America. A testimonial from fourteen officers of the *Alliance*, declaring Captain Landais to be a brave and capable commander, and a letter from the crew, saying that unless their prize-money was paid and their former captain restored to them they would not sail in the *Alliance*, accompanied the letter. Franklin deemed the send-

ing of this letter an act of unparalleled effrontery,
and in his reply frankly told its author so. At this
juncture Arthur Lee, agent of the United States at
Paris, came to the aid of our hero with an opinion
that by the terms of his old commission from Congress,
which had never been revoked, he was still lawful
commander of the *Alliance*, and indeed responsible
for her until relieved by Congress; and, with this convenient instrument in his pocket, Landais lost no time
in getting to L'Orient and regaining his old command.
Then the *Alliance* hastily completed taking in cargo
and put to sea. Arrived in Boston her captain found
the Court of Inquiry he had demanded awaiting him.
Its verdict, based solely, as its victim affirmed, on the
testimony of his enemies, was guilty of the charges
preferred by Jones, and its sentence a summary dis-
missal from the service. Degraded in rank and stained
in reputation, the Admiral returned to France and
took service under the Republic. He was at once
given command of the seventy-four-gun frigate *Patriot*,
and did efficient service in the war which the young
General Bonaparte was then waging in Italy. In
1797 he quitted the French service and returned to
New York, which continued to be his residence until
his death in 1820. These years were spent solely
in pressing his claims upon the attention of Congress.

These claims were for arrears of pay while in actual

service in the Navy, and for arrears of prize money.
The *Alliance*, while under his command, had taken
three prizes, valued in the aggregate at $40,000, which
she sent into Bergen, Norway, but which the authorities there, overawed by British power, delivered to
their former owners.   The commander's share of this
money Landais later made the basis of a heavy claim
against the Government, with what success has been
stated.   His pugnaciousness even in old age seems
not to have deserted him.   On one occasion while in
Washington, it is said, hearing that a Congressman
had spoken slightingly of him in debate, he mounted
his smallsword and proceeded to the gallery of the
House, where he despatched a page to the offending
member with an invitation to meet him on the field
of honor.   Toward Admiral John Paul Jones, whom
he regarded as the author of his misfortunes, he entertained the deepest antipathy.   The story goes —
set in motion by himself — that on one occasion he
met the Chevalier in Water Street and coolly spat in
his face — a story which was denied by Jones and his
friends as often as told.   Toward the close of his
career the Count became miserably poor, eking out
an existence by the aid of an annuity purchased years
before by his arrears of prize money.

In a memorial addressed to Congress during this
period, and later published in a pamphlet now extremely rare, he thus refers to his exploits and to the

straits to which he is reduced. The words are entirely typical of the man. He says:

"I was born and brought up in affluence; was admitted into the sea-service of the King of France in 1762, in which service I was wounded in the year 1763, in a glorious sea-battle; circumnavigated the globe under command of M. de Bougainville in the years 1766–67–68; had command of a line-of-battle ship in 1773; brought into Portsmouth, Hampshire, in 1777, a ship loaded with brass guns, mortars, etc., for the United States. Being returned to France in 1791, I had command of the French 74–gun ship *Patriot*, and had at different times under my orders ten squadrons or divisions of the army. The *Patriot* was the nearest ship to the batteries of the city of Oneglia at the taking of it. With seven ships of the line I took the Island of Antioch in 1792, which was guarded by 2500 men."

He then goes on to state that, promoted to the rank of Rear-Admiral, he had command of the ship *Ocean*, of 122 guns, on board of which his allowance for table expenses alone was forty livres per day; that he had a fortune when he came to this country, all of which had been spent in urging his claim; so that for the last seven years he had been reduced to living on a dollar a week and "when at home to do the meanest drudgery of my lodging in order to keep my honor and integrity unsoiled and to preserve my life."

The last few years of his life were spent in Brooklyn, in a house on Fulton Street. He frequented his accustomed haunts, however, so long as strength permitted. His eccentricities increased with age. He evinced much bitterness against Congress and the Government, and his sense of honor became so nice that he would not even allow a friend to pay his ferriage over the river. In 1818 he ordered a tombstone, caused to be engraved upon it the inscription given in the beginning of this paper, and then placed it at the head of his prospective grave in St. Patrick's Churchyard. When attacked by his last illness he was carried at his own request, to Bellevue Hospital, and there died September 17, 1820. After a long search I succeeded in finding the record of his death and burial in the books of the Cemetery Association, as follows:

"Admiral Peter Landais, died in Bellevue Hospital, Sept. 17, 1820. Funeral expenses $20.62½. Paid."

CHAPTER III

THERE are two interesting old cemeteries in the neighborhood of Second Avenue and Second Street, one the New York Marble Cemetery, on Second Avenue between Second and Third streets, the other the New York City Marble Cemetery on Second Street, between Second and First avenues. Although their names are similiar, they are separate organizations. Some of their features are peculiar. They are, we believe, the only cemeteries in the city whose ownership and managements are entirely non-sectarian. They are the only ones where the old-fashioned custom of interring the dead in underground vaults has always been followed. They contain the only receiving vaults in the city limits open to the general public, and their tombs hold more dust of "ancient families" than any plots of equal proportions in the town.

When they were laid out they were in a waste of pasture field; the city had then barely crept up to Bleecker Street. Now they are surrounded by piles of brick and mortar so high that the sun must be well up before its rays touch their flowers and green sward.

The New York Marble Cemetery occupies nearly all the inside, or the back yards, of the block and is entered from Second Avenue through a narrow passageway. From the iron gate on the avenue one would not imagine there was a cemetery within, for there are no monuments at all, and not even slabs to mark the exact position of the stone-lined vaults which are sunken beneath the surface. Set into the high wall surrounding the grounds are tablets bearing the names of the owners of the vaults, 156 in number. At one end is a large index tablet with the names in alphabetical order, and among them we read the well-known New York names of Kernochan, Parrish, John Hone, Scribner, Stokes, Riggs, Harvey, Van Zandt, Griswold Lorillard, Hoyt, Anthony Dey, Haggerty, and Newcomb. The grounds are laid out with three broad avenues, perhaps 200 feet long, and with cross-walks about 85 feet long at either end, and in the far corner is the receiving vault.

The New York City Marble Cemetery is in plain view of the passer-by going through Second Street. Here the vaults are 258 in number and are marked by stone slabs let into the ground, while there are many handsome monuments which have been erected by the vault owners in the memory of their dead. Against the rear wall, opposite the entrance, is a large receiving

vault, which in its day has held representatives of every
nation and clime, both the noble and ignoble, the great
and wise of the city, as well as the stranger who died
far from home and kin, within its walls. The principal
monuments and slabs bear the names of Gouverneur,
Fish, Allen, Bullus, Holt, Gallatin, Griswold, Gross,
De Klyn, Quackenbos, Kevan, Howland, and Blood-
good, Anthony, Bancker, Bergh, Bogardus, Booraem,
Hoffman, Kip, Kneeland, Lenox, Low, Morton, Ogden,
Ockershausen, Ridabock, Roosevelt, Saltus, Storm,
Tappin, Tier, Tillotson, Van Alen, Van Antwerp,
Vantine, Webb, Willett, Winans, Wynkoop, and
others.

Much more of history and romance lingers about
the old yard than the careless passer-by, or the curious
student even, at first sight would imagine. In itself
it has little claim to antiquity, having been laid out
barely seventy-six years ago. In its vaults, however,
reposes the dust of the stout old mynheers and burgo-
masters who first settled Manhattan Island. This
apparent contradiction is explained by the fact that
it has been made a receptacle for the contents of church
vaults and family burial-places among the earliest on
the island. It was first purchased in 1831 by Perkins
Nichols and Ebert A. Bancker, who designed it as a
private cemetery for their own families, and for a
limited number of others who might purchase rights
of interment there. It then formed a part of the

THE NEW YORK MARBLE CEMETERY
From a photograph taken in 1907, especially for "In Olde New York"

Phillip Minthorn farm, and the region round about was covered with farms and pastures. Bleecker Street was then on the outskirts of the city. Second Street and the adjoining avenues had been laid out, but there were no buildings on them, and a series of pastures and marshes, tenanted by geese and cattle, swept to the East River. The purchase comprised some fifteen city lots, and the sum paid was $8643. The next year, 1832, it was regularly incorporated as the New York City Marble Cemetery, the title being vested in a board of five trustees. The construction of vaults was at once begun, and 234 were completed by 1838, at which time the cemetery may be said to have been finished, although twenty-four vaults were opened in 1843. Many vaults had been purchased and many interments made before this, however, one of the first having been that of the remains of ex-President Monroe. Soon after the opening of the ground several down-town churches and many private families purchased the vaults and removed the remains of their dead thither. One of the most notable instances of this was that of the Kip family, which purchased vault 241 and removed thither generations of their dead from the old family burying-ground at Kip's Bay. About the same time the old South Dutch Church, on Garden Street, purchased vaults Nos. 191 and 192, and deposited the remains of the dead in its vaults which had lain there so long as to be unknown or unclaimed by kindred. Some 5000 dead, the trustees estimate, are now enclosed in these vaults.

Old residents of the city, familiar with the cemetery, tell of many striking scenes and incidents in its history. Imposing ceremonies attended the interment here, on the 7th of July, 1831, of the remains of James Monroe, fifth President of the United States. A brigade of militia, under General Jacob Morton, formed the military pageant. The chief men of the nation joined the procession, and, as the coffin was lowered into the vault, bells tolled, and the flags of vessels in the harbor flew at half-mast. These august ceremonies dedicated the new cemetery, so to speak, and added much to its later repute among the old, exclusive families of the city. At first thought it seems strange that Monroe, a native of Virginia, should have been interred in this little private cemetery on the outskirts of New York. The mystery becomes clear, however, when it is remembered that his son-in-law, Samuel L. Gouverneur, at whose house he died, owned a vault in the cemetery, and that it was natural for Mrs. Gouverneur to desire her father laid near her own last resting-place. After reposing here for twenty-seven years the remains were exhumed and conveyed to Virginia with rather less of ceremony than had attended their original interment. A simple incident led Virginia to take this action. Early in 1857 a number of gentlemen, natives of that State, but resident in New York, conceived the plan of raising a monument to the ex-President over the unrecognized vault that held his dust. The project was hinted abroad, and in course of time reached Virginia, where it seems to have touched State pride and jealousy to the quick. That it should be left to New York to commemorate a son of Virginia who had filled the chair of the Chief Magistrate was deemed a reflection on the Commonwealth, and steps were at once taken to have the remains removed to the State capital. To create public sentiment in favor of this, exaggerated reports as to the condition of the President's grave were spread broadcast through the State. He was reported as lying in an old, unused burying-ground, overgrown with weeds and vines, in the outskirts of the city, his grave unmarked, and cattle and hogs roaming at will above it. A committee of two was appointed by Virginia to receive the remains and attend them to their final resting-place in Hollywood Cemetery, Richmond. At the yard the exhumation was conducted with secrecy, the family being desirous of avoiding a crowd.

At 4.30 o'clock on the 2d of July, 1858, a carriage drove up to the cemetery gate. It contained Alderman Adams, representing the Common Council, and was soon joined by carriages containing the Virginia delegates, Messrs. Mumford and O. Jennings Wise, Col. James Monroe and S. L. Gouverneur representing the family, a delegation of resident Virginians, and the undertaker. At five o'clock the coffin of the ex-President was placed in the hearse, and, amid the tolling of bells, with the flags of the shipping in the harbor at half-mast, was conveyed to the Church of the Annunciation, in Fourteenth Street. Here and at the City Hall it lay in state for several days, and was then conveyed to Richmond by the steamer *Jamestown*, its escort, the famous Seventh Regiment, proceeding by the *Ericsson*. Old members of that gallant corps still remember the service for its heat and discomforts.

The visitor, perhaps, will be apt to linger longest about vaults 191 and 192. Here rest the unknown, unclaimed remains of the early burghers of New Amsterdam. What a stir you fancy there must have been among the ghosts when the edict for clearing out the vaults of the Old South went forth. A hundred and more years they had rested undisturbed. Generations had come and gone. A city had grown up around them. Their descendants, like their property, had been scattered over the earth, and now none remained to care for their bones. The church authorities, alarmed at the encroachments of the city on their property, ordered a removal to the new cemetery up town. Then came a day when the vaults were opened and the old sexton descended with his box to gather up the dust.

There are other vaults in the yard prolific of memories. In the Morton vault lie the remains of General

THE NEW YORK CITY MARBLE CEMETERY

The slab in the foreground covers the vault where James Monroe was interred. From a photograph taken in 1907, especially for "In Olde New York"

Jacob Morton, who commanded the military at the obsequies of ex-President Monroe. The receiving vault held for some years the body of the Spanish-American General Paez, who, after the usual stormy career of generals in his country, fled to New York, to find the death he had escaped in far more warlike scenes awaiting him here. The body was in dispute among the relatives, it is said, and when the question was settled it was removed to South America for burial. Commodore Eagle of the navy is buried at the west end of the yard, and near him lies Commodore Bullus; the latter, with his wife and three small children, was on board the *Chesapeake* when the *Leopard* made her murderous attack. They were on their way to a Mediterranean Consulate at the time, and during the action Mrs. Bullus and her children were removed from the cabin to a place of safety, but the Commodore, though a non-combatant, remained on deck and fought gallantly through the whole affair.

CHAPTER IV

SOME OLD-TIME FIGURES [1]

" JOHN I. BROWERE was one of a class of men
peculiar to the early days of American art. A
native of New York, he was in his youth a sign painter.
Showing promising talent, he was induced to take
lessons under Archibald Robertson, and after slight
instruction moved to Tarrytown and set up his easel
as a portrait painter, at the same time eking out his
resources by teaching school. A little later a brother
offered him a free passage to Leghorn in the ship he
commanded, and the artist proceeded to Italy, spend-
ing two years there, rambling from city to city and
diligently studying art, and more especially sculpture.
Returning to America about 1820, he built a studio
in the rear of his residence, No. 315 Broadway, adjoining the old New York Hospital, and I suppose took
the bust of every gentleman of note then living in the
city. Some 200 examples of his work are said to be
in existence in New York. His most ambitious
project was a national gallery of busts and statues of
distinguished Americans, a project encouraged by

[1] This was written in 1883.

Jefferson, Adams, Lafayette, and all the famous men of the day. Browere was a poet and inventor as well as artist; one occasionally comes upon his verses in the albums of old ladies of the city; he also invented a stove for burning anthracite coal, and a process for manufacturing oiled silk, which gave several people immense fortunes, although he, owing to his improvidence in money matters, never received a penny. He died poor in 1834, of cholera, after only six hours' illness, at his house by the old mile-stone in the Bowery, leaving his gallery only half completed. His son, A. D. O. Browere, the artist, has recently placed on exhibition a completed portion, which embraces busts of Jefferson, Lafayette, the three Adamses, Madison, Clay, DeWitt Clinton, the three captors of André, Forrest, and others."

These facts, suggested by the modest sign, "Browere's Busts of Distinguished Americans," on the front of the building No. 788 Broadway, were told me some twenty years ago by an old New Yorker. It proved to be an interesting place to visit. Climbing two flights of long winding stairs from an entrance on Tenth Street, and passing through a long passage, we entered the gallery, a well-lighted, neatly-carpeted room. Twenty-three busts were ranged around the sides, and there were others, with a collection of the exhibitor's paintings in an ante-room. The busts were interesting certainly, both as examples of the art of

1820–25 and from their historic associations, but still more interesting was the gossip and reminiscence they inspired in the white-haired gentleman who exhibited them. One might detect, however, running through his monologue a little vein of resentment at the indifference of the public to the merits of his collection, and the efforts made in certain quarters to discredit it.

"When my father was about taking the cast of Charles Carroll, of Carrollton," said he, "he received testimonials of his skill and ability from the first gentlemen in the city. I will read you this from Prof. Samuel L. Mitchell, LL.D., which was endorsed by many others equally competent to judge." From a little morocco-covered book he read: "I approve your design of executing a likeness in statuary of the Honorable Charles Carroll, of Carrollton. When you shall present yourself to him within a few days, I authorize you to employ my testimony in favor of your skill. Having submitted more than once to your plastic operations, I know that you can perform it successfully without pain and within a reasonable time. The likenesses you have made are remarkably exact; so much so that they may be called facsimile imitations of the life. Your gallery contains so many specimens of correct casts that not only committees, but critical judges, bear witness to your industry, genius, and talent."

"Jefferson writes here from Monticello, Adams from Quincy, Madison from Montpelier, Clinton from Albany, all bearing witness to the originality and life-likeness of the casts made by my father; but when at the late celebration at Tarrytown I wished to place the busts of Van Wart, Williams, and Paulding on exhibition, it was objected to by a few young artists and reporters, on the ground that it was not 'good art.' They were there, though, and an old gentleman came up who regarded them with great interest. 'Who did them?' said he at length. 'My father, John I. Browere, the sculptor,' I replied. 'I knew him and them,' he rejoined, 'and they are fine examples.' I afterward learned that the gentleman was Samuel J. Tilden.

"I want the Government to make bronze copies of the casts," he continued, "and place them in the Capitol or some museum of historical characters, but Congressmen whom I have approached say they cannot be worthy, because John I. Browere's name does not appear in Dunlap's book of American artists. I'll tell you why it does not appear. My father, before he had ever met Dunlap, was asked one day how he liked his 'Death on the Pale Horse'? 'It's a strong work,' he replied, 'but looks as if it was painted by a man with but one eye.' The remark was reported to the painter, who had but one eye, and he was mortally offended; he blackballed my father at the National Academy, and subsequently ignored him in his biographical work."

"The greatest difficulty the sculptor had in securing these," he remarked, turning to the casts, "was with Lafayette's. Of course he was very desirous of securing the distinguished friend of America for his collection, and when Lafayette visited the city in 1825 a committee of the Common Council was appointed to induce him to sit. He complied after much persuasion. The composition had set and my father was about taking it off, when the clock struck and a spectator inadvertently remarked that the hour for the corporation dinner (which Lafayette was to attend) had arrived. '*Sacre bleu!*' said he, starting up, 'take it off, take it off,' causing a piece to fall from under the eye. This accident, which necessitated a second sitting, led to some interesting correspondence preserved in my book here which you may like to read. First is a letter from the Committee of the Common Council to Lafayette, dated 'New York, Saturday, 12 o'clock, July 12, 1825,' as follows:

"'DEAR GENERAL: We have just been to see your bust by Mr. Browere, and have pleasure in saying it is vastly superior to any other likeness of General Lafayette which as yet has fallen under our inspection. Indeed it is a faithful resemblance of every part of your features and form, from the head to the breast, with the exception of a slight defect about the left eye,

caused by the loss of the material of which the mould
was made.   This defect Mr. Browere assures us (and
we have confidence in his assurance) that he can correct in a few moments and without giving you any
pain, provided you will again condescend to submit
to his operations for a limited time.   We should much
regret that the slight blemish should not be corrected,
which if not done will cause to us and to the nation a
continual source of chagrin and disappointment.'
Two days later Alderman King wrote my father:
'Every exertion has been made to get General
Lafayette to spend half an hour to get the eye of his
portrait bust completed, but in vain.   He has not had
more than four hours each night to sleep, but has
consented that you may take his mask in Philadelphia.
He left New York this morning at 8, and will be in
Philadelphia on Monday next, where he will remain
three days.   If you can be present there on Monday,
or Tuesday at furthest, you can complete the matter.
He has pledged his word.   This arrangement was all
that could be effected by your friend.'   My father,
you see, adds this postscript:

"'The subscribing artist met General Lafayette on
Monday in the Hall of Independence, Philadelphia,
and Tuesday morning from 7 to 8 was busy in making
another likeness from the face and head of the General.
At 4 P.M. of that day he finished the bust under the
eye of the General and his attendants, and had the

pleasure then of receiving from the General and his son their assurances that it was the only good bust ever made of him.'

"The masks of Jefferson, Madison, and Mrs. Madison were taken with several others during a visit to Washington made by my father in 1825. It was his custom to get a certificate of genuineness and likeness from each sitter, and there are autograph letters in this book from most of the subjects, to that effect. Jefferson, for instance, writes from Monticello, October 16, 1825: 'At the request of the Hon. James Madison, and of Mr. Browere, of the city of New York, I hereby certify that Mr. Browere has this day made a mould in plaster composition from my person for the purpose of making a portrait bust and statue for his contemplated National Gallery.' Here is a bust of Hamilton modeled from a miniature by Archibald Robertson. Jackson's bust he did not succeed in getting, as Powers had preceded him by a few days, and had extorted a promise not to sit to any other artist. He, however, made a sketch. The finest head in the collection is that of DeWitt Clinton. In appearance he was certainly the noblest Roman of them all.

"I must repeat an impromptu that Samuel Woodworth, author of 'The Old Oaken Bucket,' made on this bust. He had called to see that of Admiral Porter, and as he stood in the door on departing, father said: 'Sammy, here's something you haven't seen,' at the same time throwing off the cloth from the bust.   Woodworth made a gesture as of restraint, and repeated:

> 'Stay! the bust that graces yonder shelf
>   claims our regard.
> It is the front of Jove himself,
>   The majesty of Virtue not of Power!
> Before which Guilt and Meanness only cower.
>   Who can behold that bust and not exclaim,
> Let everlasting honor claim our Clinton's name?'

made his bow, and departed.

"Van Wart's bust my father took at Tarrytown. Paulding was brought to No. 315 by Alderman Percy Van Wyck. Williams gave him the most trouble. Twice he went by sloop and foot to Scoharie to take his mask, and both times the veteran was away from home. At length Williams came to Peekskill on a visit, General Delavan sent my father word, and he went up there and took it. This was a short time before Williams's death.   J. W. Parkinson, a gentleman of leisure in New York fifty years ago, reputed to be a natural son of George IV., once offered my father $3000 for the casts of the captors of André, his intention being to destroy them, but my father refused the offer. There is a story connected with this bust of Forrest the tragedian. There is no hair on the head, you see. When that was taken the actor was comparatively unknown, having just made his appearance in 'William Tell' at the Old Bowery Theatre. My father declared that he would make an actor of note, and asked to take his mask for his gallery. On the night the bust was taken, Forrest was to play *William Tell*, and fearing the plaster mould might cling to his hair, he donned a silk cap for the operation."

By and by, as no visitors appeared to interrupt, Mr. Browere's recollections assumed a more personal cast. He submitted to our inspection a time-stained certificate of membership in the National Academy, dated 1838, and signed by Henry Inman, President, and also a letter informing him that his picture of "Canonicus" had drawn the first Academy prize of $100. We were also shown several of his paintings, some California landscapes, and three scenes from the life of Rip Van Winkle.

CHAPTER V

ONE conversant with the history of New York knows how rapidly change has occurred in the city, but he cannot realize it vividly until he has loitered along its streets with some genial veteran who knew the town in his youth, and loves nothing better than to impart his reminiscences to the sympathetic listener. Such a walk in such company we once had the pleasure of taking, our route being down the Bowery from Astor Place to Franklin Square, and thence to the City Hall.

"All north of Astor Place, in 1825," said our companion, "was open country, a region of farms, thickets, swamps, market gardens and fine old country seats in extensive grounds. My early memories of the region beyond St. Mark's Church yonder are gruesome enough. It was then known as Stuyvesant Meadows, and gained unenviable notoriety by the hanging there of one John Johnson, whose cast, taken by Browere, may still be seen at Fowler & Wells's. Johnson was the great criminal of his day. He kept a sailor's boarding-house on Water Street, and one night murdered a farmer who had put up at his house, having, as Johnson thought, some money about him. The murderer put the remains in a sack, and was surprised, at night, carrying it through Schuyler's Alley toward the river. Guilt made him a coward. He dropped the sack and ran, its contents were thus discovered, and he was tried and sentenced by Judge Edwards to be hanged. The procession, up Broadway to Bleecker, across to the Bowery, then down Ninth Street to the gallows, called out the greatest crowd New York had ever seen, and led to the abolition of such displays. Johnson was attired for the occasion in white, with a white cap drawn over his head. He rode in an open carriage escorted by Stewart's troop of cavalry in advance, and a detachment of the National Guard in the rear, while an immense crowd of all ages and both sexes followed."

We had now progressed as far down the Bowery as Bleecker Street. "Bleecker was my great blackberry preserve when I was a boy," observed our cicerone, with a sigh. "What luscious berries grew beside the walls on either side, and roses — no such roses bloom nowadays." A few doors below Bleecker, he stopped opposite a beer saloon. "Right here Charlotte Temple lived after her retirement from the stage, and died here. The house was one story high, with two dormer-windows and a trellis on both sides covered with the luxuriant vines of the trumpet-flower.

There was a little yard in front about twenty feet deep filled with shrubs and flowers. The house was a Mecca for the good and gifted of the city so long as its mistress resided there, and few strangers of distinction came to the city without paying a visit there. It was known for some time after her death as the 'Temple House,' and finally was turned into a drinking saloon called the Gotham.

"The Bowery in those days resembled a country road; it was unpaved and sandy above Spring Street, and was studded pretty thickly with residences of the gentry. These had high stoops fronting the road, and were embowered in trees and shrubbery. Many a summer night I have seen whole families on the stoops enjoying the cool of the evening, and children trundling hoops or playing marbles on the sidewalk. There was one institution peculiar to the Bowery in those days, or at least it attained greater perfection there than in other parts of the city. I refer to the hot-corn venders. These were exclusively colored women, each dressed as neatly as though she had come out of a bandbox, with a flaming bandanna handkerchief on her head tied in a peak, West India fashion, the ends hanging down, and clean white or checked apron. They sat on stools at the street corners and noted places, each with a pail beside her, filled with hot corn on the ear, and a small cup on each side, one containing salt and the other butter. When a patron approached she handed

him a smoking ear, and the salt and butter; the latter
he gravely rubbed on the ear and ate as he stood.
Their cry was musical, and could be heard blocks
away. 'Hot corn, hot corn! here's your lily white
hot corn,' they cried, but an old woman who sold on
the corner of Hester and Bond Streets, improved on
this. Her cry was:

> 'Hot corn, hot corn!
> Some for a penny and some two cents.
> Corn cost money and fire expense,
> Here's your lily-white hot corn!'

"There were almost as many venders on the streets
then as now, but more characteristic and picturesque.
Some bore trays containing baked pears swimming
in molasses, which the purchaser took between his
thumb and finger and ate. The 'sand man' was a
verity in those days. All the barrooms, restaurants,
and many of the kitchens in the city had sanded floors,
and men in long white frocks, with two-wheeled carts,
peddling Rockaway sand, were familiar objects on
the streets. Then there were the darkeys who sold
bundles of straw for filling beds, and an old blind
man who sold door-mats made of picked tar rope.
One of the most genial and popular landlords in the
city I have seen peddling pails of pure spring water
in the Bowery at two cents a pail. He brought it from
what was then called Greenwich Village, above Aaron
Burr's Richmond Hill mansion.

"This is the most distinctive landmark of old New York I have seen," he remarked when another block was passed, patting affectionately as he spoke a mossy old mile-stone set in the sidewalk nearly opposite Rivington Street, which bore this legend, "1 Mile from City Hall." "Many a tired passenger in the four-horse tally-ho six days on the road from Boston has gleefully hailed this stone. The drivers of the Harlem and Manhattanville stages always greeted it with a merrier bugle peal. In those days we hadn't thought of a railroad, and the Erie Canal was just being opened. Spring Street marked the limits of the paved streets in this direction when I was a boy and young man. The walks were mostly of bricks laid cat-a-cornered, in those days.

"You see that third house on the side street. There I found my wife. I was passing one morning and saw her through the window looking down the street. Suddenly she became aware that I was staring at her, and slammed the blind to with energy. 'Sam,' said I to my brother, 'that girl's going to be my wife.' Passing that way a few days after, I saw a notice out that boarders would be taken, and presented myself as a candidate. Six months after we were married. That is fifty years ago, and I have never had cause to regret it; she has been a good wife.

"I never cross Grand Street"— we had reached the roar and rush of that thoroughfare — "without

thinking of a walk I had down it to the ferry in 1823.
There was to be a race that day on a course near
where the Union course was opened later, and all
New York interested in sport went out there to see it.
The race was between Eclipse and Sir Henry, and the
great interest taken in it arose from the fact that it had
been arranged between the horsemen of the North
and South to test the merits of the thoroughbreds of
the two sections.   Eclipse represented the North and
Sir Henry the South.   There was not a house on Grand
Street then between Essex Street and the ferry.   I saw
on the south wild marshy pasture fields, with cattle
grazing among the black berry and wild-rose bushes,
and in the distance on the hills some old Dutch farmhouses.   Colonel Willet's place, on the left, a fine old
country mansion, I remember, standing back from
the road amid its orchards.   Grand Street Ferry was
then known as the 'Hook' ferry.   You would laugh
at the ferry-boats of those days.   They had open
decks with an awning stretched over and benches
around the sides, and were propelled by horse-power.
From four to sixteen horses were required, and they
walked around a shaft in the center of the boat, turning it as sailors turn the capstan, and this shaft by
gearing turned the paddle wheels.   On some boats
the horses worked a tread mill like the modern thresh-
ing machines.   The North triumphed that day —
Eclipse won.   I doubt if he would, however, had it

not been for Sam Purdy, a noted jockey of that time.
Eclipse lost the first heat, and Purdy saw from his
place on the judge's stand that his jockey was goring
him so terribly that he bled. So he leaped from the
stand, pulled the jockey off, and mounted in his place.
Eclipse felt the change at once, put his head up and
tail out and won the next two heads easily, putting
$20,000 in his master's pocket."

Chatham Square and Franklin Square recalled many
reminiscences, but not of a nature to interest the
public. In City Hall Park, however, our friend's
recollections became of more general interest. "The
City Hall had just been built then, between two prisons,
the Bridewell and jail. The jail, or debtor's prison,
was east of the hall and surrounded with a tight board
fence about eight feet high. On the Chambers Street
side of the Park were three buildings, all under one
roof. First (nearest Broadway) was the American
or Scudder's Museum, then the Academy of Fine
Arts, and the Almshouse, the artist and showman
being not far from the Almshouse at that day in more
senses than one. John Vanderlyn's Rotunda came
next on the east. Vanderlyn had been discovered by
Colonel Burr, in an interior town, covering his master's
blacksmith's shop with charcoal sketches, and had
been sent by him to Paris and Rome for education in
art. His 'Marius amid the ruins of Carthage' had
taken the prize at Paris under Napoleon, and he re-

turned to New York comparatively famous. The city, thinking to do something for American art, built the Rotunda and gave Vanderlyn the lease of it for a studio, and for the exhibition of his pictures. He exhibited there his 'Marius,' 'Ariadne,' and the 'Garden of Versailles,' the latter a panorama taking up two sides of the room. Speaking of pictures, Michael Paff once made a lucky discovery. Paff was a picture dealer, having a store on Broadway, near Vesey, and the best art connoisseur in the city. A gentleman in town had a large picture of Esther before King Ahasuerus, that he had secured at an auction sale, and which his wife was desirous of exchanging for two landscapes at Paff's. Paff good-naturedly made the exchange, but in cleaning up his new purchase discovered it to be a genuine Van Dyck. After that he spent about a week to the square inch cleaning and bringing out the original color. Wealthy gentlemen, art patrons, would drop in during the process, and offer to purchase. Paff's first price was $1000, after that he rose $1000 on every offer not accepted. Lyman Reid, the patron of Cole, offered him $7000 for it, which was quickly rejected, Paff's price having then risen to $16,000. I was in the store one day with Alfred Pell and Lyman Reid when Sir Robert Porter came in and offered Paff $12,000 for the picture, saying he was authorized to give that sum and no more by the National Gallery, of London. Paff refused, and held on to the

BROADWAY, LOOKING SOUTHWARD FROM CITY HALL PARK

This part of City Hall Park is now occupied by the Post Office building. From an old lithographic print in the collection of John D. Crimmins of New York

picture till his death. After that event, his widow
sold the picture to the National Gallery, it was said,
for $20,000. I could give you a volume of reminis-
cences about the old American Museum. It had been
removed to the site of the later *Herald* Building,
and had ruined several owners, when P. T. Barnum
got hold of it and made a success of it.

"A fence surrounded the Park in those days, with
an entrance gate on the west. On the Chatham Street
side were a number of low one-story buildings —
cigar shops, beer saloons, and the pawn-shop of William
Stevenson, the first of the kind ever opened in New
York. Right opposite, on the corner of Frankfort
Street, stood Tammany Hall, the cradle of the present
famous organization; the modern sachems, you will
reflect, were but papooses then. The Hall was used
chiefly for public meetings of a political cast. The
real council-room of the braves was a saloon a hundred
feet back on Frankfort Street, called the 'Pewter Mug.'
Here the chiefs held their pow-wows, and the plan
of their campaigns was mapped out. Several lawyers
of note had offices in the Hall. Aaron Burr's was on
the south side of the building. Many a time have I
seen him help Madame Jumel into her carriage standing before the door, and he did it with incomparable
grace."

CHAPTER VI

SOME OLD BOOKSELLERS

OF the many obscure callings by which men gain a livelihood in New York none is more useful than that of the antiquarian booksellers, of whom there were in 1885 about twenty in the city. The favorite home of this class was then the region traversed by William and Nassau streets, which may be said to be bounded somewhat indefinitely, by Cliff Street on the east and Broadway on the west.

These establishments displayed no gilded signs or plate-glass windows to the public gaze. They never advertised in the public prints; they rather avoided than sought publicity, being hidden away in musty, ill-smelling apartments, up many flights of narrow stairs, or at the end of long, dimly-lighted passages. Their customers in person were few, their chief patrons being the collectors and bibliophiles of the entire country, and these were reached by catalogues issued quarterly. These catalogues were often extensive and elaborate, and displayed much wit and ingenuity in their construction. The first page of a catalogue of 1868, for instance, reads as follows:

"Two thousand seven hundred personals, funeral sermons, eulogies, biographical sketches, memorials, &c., which may be bought — if any one wants them — of ——, who, on receipt of the trifling number of cents hinted at just to the left of the place and date of imprint will take pleasure in sending any one or more of them, at his own expense, to any place where Uncle Sam keeps a post-office."

The "Motto" is the following sentiment from Horace Greeley:

"A man who does not care enough about his relations to pay four shillings for a funeral sermon on his grandfather, or even on his mother-in-law, is a born ingrate, and meaner than a goat thief."

Another is a "catalogue of about two bushels of tidbits relating to that never-to-be-forgotten scrimmage the American Revolution, for sale by ——, book peddler." In his preface to the same the old bookseller thus refers to some of the bores that infect a bookseller's shop:

"At the instance of a considerable number of friendly critics who have heretofore more than made up by their willingness to give good advice for their reluctance to buy anything, but who without doubt are only waiting for me to show a proper and becoming appreciation of their views, I have requested the printer to put the A's at one end of this list and the W's at another, and call it a catalogue. As I am now for the first time trying to cater to a class of pundits who know what's what, I have not ventured to apply the terms rare and scarce, nor any one of the endless changes which may be rung upon them by the hand of a master. I trust, however, that I shall be pardoned (as I have a family to support) for mentioning that a considerable number of my tidbits were considered by Mr. Stevens worthy a place in his catalogue of nuggets, and that not a few of them are so uncommon that they have escaped the notice of the compiler of that invaluable handbook, Sabin's Dictionary, and his hundred-eyed corps of assistants. Perhaps — as is constitutional with me — I have been modester than I could afford, and that I ought to have made an unsparing use of the adjectives and peppered my book with them, hit or miss. The die is cast, however; quite likely I may not sell a tidbit; but I am determined this once to give my modesty the rein, and like Lord Timothy Dexter, let critic or customer pepper or salt this, my first catalogue, to suit himself.

"Having chosen my exemplar, I will be no less attentive to the convenience of my critics and customers than was his Lord Timothyship to the wants of his readers. I have therefore copied for their use, from a recent auction catalogue, a few of the adjectives and persuasives applied to such of the commoner tidbits as the owner had been able to 'buy at a bargain.' 'Scarce,' 'Very scarce,' 'Rare,' 'Very Rare,'

"Tres Rare' (that's French). 'Unattainable except at public sale.' 'Not mentioned by Rich.' 'We have never sold a copy.' 'We are unable to record any other copy.'"

The immense private collections which are from time to time unloaded upon the market hurt the trade and are greatly dreaded by the old booksellers. Such a collection was the Brinley library, sold at auction in New York.

In his catalogue, issued soon after the sale, one of the tradesmen thus labors with the deluded buyers who will purchase at auction rather than of the trade:

"This sale footed up nearly $49,000. Mr. Brinley, by his will, not less wisely than generously, gave to five public libraries $24,500, to be bought out or, as a book-peddler would express it, in trade.

"The libraries of the favored institutions fought nobly. So nobly that it is doubtful if the bequests will make the estate a dollar the poorer. Of books so rare that I know nothing about their value, I will say as little as I know. Rare books that I had seen sold before, sold high. The greater part of the catalogue sold very high. Hundreds of common books — so common that they may readily be found in bookstores, and yet not unworthy a place in this splendid collection — sold at prices far beyond what any bookseller would dare to ask. Buyers of such, except 'on account,' generally got their fingers burnt. I had myself just enough of that sort of experience to know how it feels. Having by mistake bought lot 1785 for $15, I had it resold on my account; it brought $7. At the reselling the librarians did not rally worth a cent. I would have cheerfully given their institutions a dollar apiece all round if they had stood by me.

"Lot 163, Chalmers Annals, found an appreciative buyer at $18.50. I sold the young gentleman from the country, who bid $18, a much better copy the next morning for half the money. The same buyer secured lot 176, Phillips's Paper Currency, at $7.50. I can generally furnish it at five, ten off to public libraries. I may leave them nothing by will, but mean to do my level best by them as long as I live.

"Lot 205, Trumbull's United States, somebody must have been in a great hurry for. It brought $3. The next bidder is my affinity, if I could only find him. I should be happy to sell him a clean, uncut copy for a dollar.

"Lot 234, Knox's Journal, lacking a portrait and a title-page, was snapped up at $16. I have a copy which could be made as good as Mr. Brinley's by pulling out a title-page — it already fills the bill in lacking a portrait — which I am dying to sell for ten.

"No. 289, Drake's Address, sold for $2. If the previous bidder will send a small boy with seventy-five cents he will get a copy by return boy.

"No. 325, Lechford,— $2.75. I have a few more

left of the same sort at $1.50.   No. 374, Noah Web-
ster's version of Winthrop's Journal, $10.   I sold as
good a copy not long since at $4.   Numbers 267 and
390, Commissionary Wilson's Orderly Book and
Easton's King Philip, as it is called for short, are numbers I. and II. of Munsell's Historical Series, in 10
volumes, which during the large paper and limited
edition mania used to sell as high as $400 per set.
The two volumes brought $26.50.   A complete set in
half morocco will be found in this catalogue at $35.

"No. 331, Papers Concerning the Attack on Hatfield
and Deerfield, wiped out sixteen of the ten thousand
dollars given to Yale College.   It used to sell at a
much higher figure, but times have changed.   I sold a
copy a short time ago for five.

"No. 412, News from New England, 2 copies, both
found purchasers at $2.25.   I have a copy, see my
No. 274, at seventy-five cents.

"No. 767, James Fitch's Connecticut Election
Sermon, Cambridge, 1674, the first printed, sold for
$38.   In a note to lot 2154 Dr. Trumbull, the cata-
loguer, says: 'Five [Conn. Election] sermons were
printed in Cambridge and Boston before a press was
established in Connecticut.   Of these five, four will
be found elsewhere in this catalogue.'   That's so, and
the four, which were the first, third, fourth and fifth,
brought an average of $25.50 each.   In the same note
Dr. Trumbull, whose notes are always interesting,

says further: 'Mr. Brinley began this collection nearly forty years ago, and allowed no opportunity of completing and perfecting it to escape.' I sold a beautiful copy of the one which Mr. Brinley did not have a short time ago for $15. I always sent my catalogue to the gentlemen who bought the other four, but buyers at auction of course save the book-peddlers' profit.

"Of numbers 975, 1029, 50, 81, 96 and 1117, 'Mathers,' good copies will be found in this catalogue at peddlers' prices. Numbers 1356, 7, Drake's Witchcraft Delusion, small and large paper, sold for $9.00 and $10.50 in paper. I sell them at five and six. No. 1359, Drake's Annals of Witchcraft, sold for $8.75 in cloth. I sell it for $2.50 in paper. Another half dollar would buy a cloth jacket for it, leaving nearly two-thirds of the money toward buying the buyer a jacket.

"No. 1377 was bought by the author for $2.25. For the money I would have given him three copies. I catalogue it at seventy-five cents and always send him my catalogues.

"I have an indistinct recollection of having in my early youth read a short list of conundrums, each one of which was too much for an eastern king whose reputation for wisdom stood high. Had Solomon — I think that was the king's name — attended the Brinley sale I am convinced that in his list of things which no fellow can find out would be ranked as the knottiest the question why book-buyers in bookshops are so stingy and in book auctions so lavish."

There are specialists, even among the dealers in dead books, one being known to his fellows as dealing largely in genealogies and kindred works; another makes a specialty of rare foreign books and prints; another confines himself to rare Americana; while a fourth devotes his energies exclusively to the collection and sale of American pamphlets. A chance service rendered one of the guild, in the discovery of a rare volume, gained me his good will, a seat at his fireside, and a share in the racy anecdotes with which he enlivened it; these anecdotes covered a wide range of subjects, and included reminiscences of the famous literary men of two generations who had frequented his shop. Some of these reminiscences I am sure will interest the reader.

Of Poe he said: "The character drawn of Poe by his various biographers and critics may with safety be pronounced an excess of exaggeration, but this is not to be much wondered at when it is considered that these men were his rivals, either as poets or prose-writers, and it is well known that such are generally as jealous of each other as are the ladies who are handsome of those who desire to be considered so. It is an old truism, and as true as it is old, that in the multitude of counsellors there is safety. I therefore will show you my opinion of this gifted but unfortunate genius: it may be estimated as worth little, but it has this merit: It comes from an eye- and ear-witness, and this, it must be remembered, is the very highest of legal evidence. For eight months or more, 'one house contained us, us one table fed.' During that time I saw much of him, and had an opportunity of conversing with him often; and I must say I never saw him the least affected with liquor, nor ever descend to any known vice, while he was one of the most courteous, gentlemanly and intelligent companions I have ever met. Besides, he had an extra inducement to be a good man, for he had a wife of matchless beauty and loveliness; her eye could match that of any houri, and her face defy the genius of a Canova to imitate; her temper and disposition were of surpassing sweetness; in addition, she seemed as much devoted to him and his every interest as a young mother is to her first-born. During this time he wrote his longest prose romance, entitled the *Adventures of Arthur Gordon Pym*. Poe had a remarkably pleasing and prepossessing countenance — what the ladies would call decidedly handsome. He died after a brief and fitful career at Baltimore, October, 1849, where his remains lie interred in an obscure burying-ground."

Of Simms he showed this entry in his diary, under date of October 15, 1868: "To-day I had the pleasure of a call from William Gilmore Simms, the novelist. He is quite affable in conversation, and apparently

well stocked with general information, which he can
impart with fluency. He appears somewhat down-
cast, or rather, I should say, has a melancholy cast of
countenance: he is advanced in years, with a profusion
of hair around his face, chin and throat — is apparently
between sixty and seventy years of age. I requested
him to enroll his name in my autograph-book, which
he did with readiness. He remarked that he was
often requested to do so, especially by the ladies. I
replied that this was a debt which every man incurred
when he became public property either by his words,
actions, or writings. He acquiesced in the justice of
the remark. Mr. Simms was in search of a copy of
Johnson's *History of the Seminoles*, to aid him in
making a new book. He was accompanied by Mr.
Duykinck."

Halleck he thus introduced: "On a certain occasion
I was passing a Roman Catholic church in New York:
seeing the doors open and throngs of people pressing
in, I stepped inside to see what I could see. I had not
well got inside when I beheld Fitzgreene Halleck
standing uncovered, with reverential attitude, among
the crowd of unshorn and unwashed worshipers. I
remained till I saw him leave. In doing so he made a
courteous bow, as is the polite custom of the humblest
of these people on taking their departure.

"On the subject of compliments paid him for poeti-
cal talents, Mr. Halleck once said to me, 'They are

generally made by those who are ignorant or who
have a desire to please or flatter, or perhaps a combination of all.   As a general thing, they are devoid
of sincerity, and rather offensive than pleasing.   There
is no general rule without its exception, however, and
in my bagful of compliments I cherish one which comes
under that rule, and reflecting upon it affords me real
pleasure as it did then.   On a warm day in summer
a young man came into the office with a countenance
glowing with ardor, innocence, and honesty, and his
eyes beaming with enthusiasm. Said he, "Is Mr.
Halleck to be found here?" I answered in the affirma-
tive.   Continued he, with evidently increased emotion,
"Could I see him?" — "You see him now," I replied.
He grasped me by the hand with a hearty vigorousness
that added to my conviction of his sincerity.   Said he,
"I am happy, most happy, in having had the pleasure
at last of seeing one whose poems have afforded me no
ordinary gratification and delight. I have longed to
see you, and I have dreamt that I have seen you, but
now I behold you with mine own eyes.   God bless
you for ever and ever! I have come eleven hundred
miles, from the banks of the Miami in Ohio, mainly
for that purpose, and I have been compensated for
my pains."'

"Mr. Halleck told me that he had been solicited to
write a life of his early and beloved friend Drake.
'But,' said he, 'I did not well see how I could grant

such a request: I had no lever for my fulcrum. What could I say about one who had studied pharmacy, dissection, written a few poems, and then left the scene of action? I had no material, and a mere meaningless eulogy would have been out of the question.'

"In personal appearance Halleck was rather below the medium height and well built: in walking he had a rather slow and shuffling gait, as if something afflicted his feet; a florid, bland, and pleasant countenance; a bright gray eye; was remarkably pleasant and courteous in conversation, and, as a natural consequence, much beloved by all who had the pleasure of his acquaintance. But to that brilliancy in conversation which some of his admirers have been pleased to attribute to him, in my opinion he could lay no claim. His library was sold at auction in New York on the evening of October 12, 1868. If the collection disposed of on that occasion was really his library in full, it must be confessed it was a sorry affair and meager in the extreme. In surveying the collection a judge of the value of such property would perhaps pronounce it worth from one hundred and twenty-five to one hundred and fifty dollars. The books brought fabulous prices — at least ten times their value. The company was large, good-humored, and just in the frame of mind to be a little more than liberal, doubtless stimulated to be so from a desire to possess a relic of the departed poet who had added fame to the literature of his country. The following are the names of a few of the books and the prices they brought: *Nicholas Nickleby*, with the author's autograph, $18; Bryant's little volume of poems entitled *Thirty Poems*, with the author's autograph, $11; Campbell's *Poems*, with Halleck's autograph, $8.50; *Catalogue of the Strawberry Hill Collection*, $16; *Barnaby Rudge*, presentation copy by the author to Halleck, $15; Coleridge's *Poems*, with a few notes by Halleck, $10; *Fanny*, a poem by Mr. Halleck, $10. The sum-total realized for his library was twelve hundred and fifty dollars."

Aaron Burr was the subject of some interesting reminiscences: "Shortly after I came to New York, Aaron Burr was pointed out to me as he was slowly wending his way up Broadway, between Chambers Street and the old theater, on the City Hall side. I frequently afterward met him in this and other streets. He was always an object of interest, inasmuch as he had become an historical character, somewhat notoriously so. I will attempt to describe his appearance, or rather how he appeared to me: He was small, thin and attenuated in form, perhaps a little over five feet in height, weight not much over a hundred pounds. He walked with a slow, measured and feeble step, stooping considerably, occasionally with both hands behind his back. He had a keen face and deep-set, dark eye, his hat set deep on his head, the back part sunk down to the collar of the coat and the back brim somewhat turned upward. He was dressed in threadbare black cloth, having the appearance of what is known as shabby genteel. His countenance wore a melancholy aspect, and his whole appearance betokened one dejected, forsaken, forgotten or cast aside, and conscious of his position. He was invariably alone when I saw him, except on a single occasion: that was on the sidewalk in Broadway fronting what is now the Astor House, where he was standing talking very familiarly with a young woman whom he held by one hand. His countenance on that occasion was cheerful, lighted up and bland — altogether different from what it appeared to me when I saw him alone and in conversation with himself. Burr must have been a very exact man in his business-affairs. His receipt-book came into my possession. I found there receipts for a load of wood, a carpenter's work for one day, a pair of boots, milk for a certain number of weeks, suit of clothes, besides numerous other small transactions that but few would think of taking a receipt for. The book was but a sorry, cheap affair, and could not have cost when new more than fifty cents."

Edwin Forrest he thus mentioned: "At the time when Forrest was earning his reputation on the board of the Bowery Theatre I was connected with that institution, and of course had an opportunity of seeing him every night he performed. Mr. Forrest appeared to be possessed of the perfection of physical form, more especially conspicuous when arrayed in some peculiar costumes which tended to display it to the best advantage. He had a stentorian voice, and must have had lungs not less invulnerable than one of Homer's heroes. He had a fine masculine face and prepossessing countenance, much resembling many of the notable Greeks and Romans whose portraits have come down to our time, and a keen intellectual eye. His countenance at times assumed an air of hauteur which doubtless had become a habit, either from personating characters of this stamp or from a consciousness of his merited popularity. He left the impression on the beholder of one intoxicated with success and the repletion of human applause. He kept aloof from all around him, and condescended to no social intercourse with any one on the stage, and appeared to entertain a contempt for his audience. . . . He has now lost that mercurial, youthful appearance which was then so conspicuous, and which doubtless aided in laying the foundation of his widespread reputation. He was then straight as an arrow and elastic as a circus-rider, the very beau-ideal of physical perfection: now he bears the marks of decay, or rather, as is said of grain just before harvest, he has a ripe appearance. If he would consult his renown he would retire from the stage, and never set foot upon it again."

The reminiscences also touched on Bryant, Parton, Mrs. Siddons and several eminent divines and journalists. Of the latter class the fullest related to James Gordon Bennett, founder of the *Herald*, and his coadjutor, William H. Attree. "I remember entering the subterranean office of Mr. Bennett early in the career of the *Herald* and purchasing a single copy of the paper, for which I paid the sum of one cent only. On this occasion the proprietor, editor, and vendor was seated at his desk busily engaged in writing, and appeared to pay little or no attention to me as I entered. On making known my object in coming in, he requested me to put my money down on the counter and help myself to a paper: all the time he continued his writing operations. The office was a single, oblong, underground room. Its furniture consisted of a counter, which also served as a desk, constructed from two flour-barrels, perhaps empty, standing apart from each other about four feet, with a single plank covering both; a chair, placed in the center, upon which sat the editor busy at his vocation, with an inkstand by his right hand; on the end nearest the door were placed the papers for sale. I attribute the success of the *Herald* to a combination of circumstances — to the peculiar fitness of its editor for his position, to its cheapness, and its advertising patronage, which was considerable. In the fourth place, it early secured the assistance of William II. Attree, a man of uncom-

mon abilities as a reporter and a concocter of pithy
as well as ludicrous chapters greatly calculated to
captivate many readers. In fact, this clever and
talented assistant in some respects never had his match.
He did not, as other reporters do, take down in short-
hand what the speaker or reader said, but sat and
heard the passing discourse like any other casual
spectator: when over he would go home to his room,
write out in full all that had been said on the occasion,
and that entirely from memory. On a certain occasion I hinted to him my incredulity about his ability
to report as he had frequently informed me. To put
the matter beyond doubt, he requested me to accompany him to Clinton Hall to hear some literary mag-
nate let off his intellectual steam. I accordingly
accompanied him as per arrangement. We were
seated together in the same pew. He placed his hands
in his pockets and continued in that position during
the delivery of the discourse, and when it was finished
he remarked to me that I would not only find the sub-
stance of this harangue in the *Herald* the next day,
but that I would find it word for word. On the following morning I procured the paper, and read the report
of what I had heard the previous evening; and I must
say I was struck with astonishment at its perfect
accuracy. Before Mr. Attree's time reporting for the
press in New York was a mere outline or sketch of
what had been said or done, but he infused life and

soul into his department of journalism. His reports were full, accurate, graphic; and, what is more, he frequently flattered the vanity of the speaker by making a much better speech for him than he possibly could for himself. Poor Attree died in 1849, and is entombed at Greenwood."

CHAPTER VII

A NEW YORK CURIOSITY SHOP

IT was kept by a descendant of one of the old island families, and his stock was confined almost entirely to relics, coats of arms, pedigrees, and other souvenirs of the early Dutch families of Manhattan. The most striking feature observed on entering was the array of tall eight-day clocks extending around the four sides of the room, in some places two ranks deep. The cases were mostly of oak, beautifully inlaid, and which bore on the base the coat of arms, and in some instances the name, of the family for whom they were made. Beekman, Kouwenhoven, Leiter, Van Westervelt, Brower, Van Hardenburgh, Weber, De Groot, Prevoorst, Schermerhorn, and Van Wyck, were the most prominent names noticed. There were thirty of these clocks — two of great historical interest. All were of heavy and elaborate workmanship, and, besides the carving and inlaid work on the cases, were prettily decorated on the arch above the face with vines and flowers. Most had eight astronomical movements, giving, in addition to the hour, minute, and second, the day of the month and week, the phases of sun and

moon, and the sign of the zodiac. Some also gave the
evening and morning star, and nearly all had the
alarm movement.

The Moll or Maule clock by the door was the most
valuable of all the stock, historically considered. On
the 10th of July, 1680, John Moll, a Swede, received
from the Indians of Delaware a deed for much of the
land now comprising Delaware and Eastern Pennsylvania. This he subsequently conveyed to William
Penn. From timber cut on this tract he made, or had
made, the case of this old clock, now standing so
modestly in the corner, and sent it to his relatives, the
Maule family in Holland, as a present from the New
World to the Old. They valued it so highly that they
had the family arms inlaid in the solid oak, and decorated it very prettily with vines, leaves, and birds of
plumage; furthermore, to show its American origin,
they had impaled in the arms the names of the six
Indian chiefs from whom John Moll had made his
purchase. The shop-keeper who goes every year to
the cities of Holland and Germany to replenish his
stock chanced to catch sight of the arms on the clock
as he was mousing about a second-hand store in
Amsterdam and purchased it.

Another very notable clock was that on which
Christopher Huggins experimented in the invention
of the pendulum. Huggins, as the legend is, was an
ingenious clock-maker of Amsterdam in 1689, who

gave so much time to evolving his idea of the pendulum
that he got into financial straits, and borrowed 600
guilders of Jacobus Van Wyck, a wealthy manufac-
turer of clocks and watches in that city.   The inventor,
however, was never able to pay the debt, and so turned
the clock over to his creditor.   To prove that this is
the identical clock the owner points to the letters " C.
H. to J. V. W." engraved on the metal frame.   The
mechanism has but one hand, and is a quaint array
of wheels and chains.

There was much other furniture of rare and curious
interest — carved, stiff-backed chairs with figured
cushions, square and half-round tables, sideboards,
secretaries, all of solid oak, quaintly carved and richly
inlaid.   A wardrobe, the largest piece of furniture in
the room, seven feet high and as many wide, has a
curious history.   Without and within it contains no
less than ten thousand pieces of inlaid work, and was
made by the Guild of Cabinet Workers of Amsterdam
and presented to Nicholas Oppermier, Burgomaster of
that city from 1681 to 1684.   A writing-desk and bureau
combined was of interest from having once belonged
to the Coxe family, who came over with William Penn.
The family arms — a sheaf of wheat or, on a green
field — is inlaid on the lid.   There was an ancient
looking-glass, too, with a carved frame and long arms
on either side, furnished at their extremities with candle-
sticks in order that the glass might be serviceable by

night as well as by day.   Two groups of rare old china
on a shelf would attract the attention of collectors.
The first group is the identical teapot, milk pitcher,
and cup — plain, rather coarse ware — used by the
first Napoleon in his campaigns — at least the merchant
who owns it was so assured by the old servant of
Joseph Bonaparte, King of Holland and brother of
Napoleon, of whom he bought them.   The only
ornament is the initial N. on a blue ground surrounded
by a coronet.   The companion group which belonged
to Joseph Bonaparte is much prettier; the ware is
finer, more delicate, and the white ground is relieved
by blue figures.

There were several notable portraits in the collection.
One of these was a very ancient portrait of Calvin,
picked up for a trifle in an old picture store, but which
the merchant, by comparison with several authentic
portraits in Europe, had established to be genuine.
Another was the only portrait in existence of Jan Jans,
father of the celebrated Ancke Jans, and the last survivor of the famous siege of Haarlem.   There was
the picture too of a modest round-faced comely Quaker
lady, in a plain brown dress, with a white handkerchief
thrown carelessly over her head, the wife of William
Penn.   "Penn was partly of Dutch extraction," the
merchant remarked, referring to the portrait, "his
father, Admiral Penn, having married a member of
the old Dutch family of Callowhill.   Callowhill Street,

in Philadelphia, is named after her." There was also a portrait of De Groot, and a strong picture of an old nude man by Barneveldt. The merchant showed also the genealogical records of eighty-six thousand Dutch and Belgian families, a part of his business being the construction of family records.

CHAPTER VIII

THE OLD JUMEL MANSION[1]

VISITORS to High Bridge — the pretty little village which stands at the northern limit of Manhattan Island — cannot have failed to observe the stately, somewhat antiquated mansion standing in the midst of a pretty park of some fifty acres, and overlooking city and river and the varied Westchester plains. It is the chief in point of interest as it is the sole survivor of the many historic houses that once graced the island, but is so environed with city encroachments and improvements that its destruction seems likely to be but a question of time. Even now the shrill whistle of the metropolitan locomotives is heard beneath its eaves. Tenth Avenue passes but a block away, and eager speculators have staked out city lots at its very gates, so hardly is it pressed by the great city in its eager outreaching for new territory.

Few persons who pass the place know, perhaps, the many points of historic and romantic interest that it has: how it occupies historic ground, being built on

[1] Written about 1880. The old mansion is now owned by the Daughters of the Revolution and maintained as a Museum.

the far-famed Harlem Heights, within a mile of the
site of old Fort Washington; that it was built for the
dower of a lady of such beauty and grace that she was
able to win the heart of the Father of his Country
himself; that within its walls Washington established
his headquarters while the mastery of the island was
in dispute with the British, and that thither Washington came again in 1790 with all his Cabinet, on his
return from a visit to the battlefield of Fort Washington; or that afterward, a once famous Vice-President
of the United States was married in its parlors. Yet
these and many other noteworthy incidents in its history are quite within the line of research of the industrious investigator. It will not be time misspent, perhaps, if we devote an idle hour to a more particular
narration of some of these events in its history.

In 1756 no belle in New York society was more
courted and caressed than Miss Mary Phillipse. She
was the daughter of Frederick Phillipse, lord of the
manor of Phillipsburg (now Yonkers), and is admitted
to have been one of the most beautiful and charming
women of colonial times.

Washington, during one of his frequent visits to the
city, met her at the house of his friend Beverly Robin-
son, and was so deeply smitten with her charms that,
if the old traditions are correct, he became a suitor for
her hand.

A rival claimant for the hand of Miss Phillipse was

THE JUMEL MANSION IN 1854

Washington's Headquarters in 1776, and the home of Colonel Roger Morris. From a Valentine's Manual (1854) print in the collection of John D. Crimmins of New York

Roger Morris, a gallant captain in the British army
then garrisoning New York. The reader's sympathies are with the young Virginian no doubt, but it was
remarked by the gossips of the day that he was a slow
wooer, and that the odds seemed in favor of his more
ardent rival, when, unfortunately, the exigencies of
Indian warfare called him to the frontier, and he was
forced to depart, leaving the gallant captain in undis-
puted possession of the field. When he had been
absent some months a friend in New York (whether
in the confidence of the lady or not is not known)
wrote to him that " Morris was laying close siege to
Miss Phillipse," and that if he had any interests in that
quarter he could best serve them by a visit to the city
— a bit of friendly advice which was not accepted,
possibly because the recipient was too much occupied
with measures for the protection of the frontier, but
probably because his chances of success seemed too
small to warrant the venture.

In the meantime, his rival out of the field, Captain
Morris, pressed his suit with military ardor, and so
successfully that in 1756 the polite society of the town
was pleasantly electrified by the news of the betrothal
of Captain Roger Morris to Mary Phillipse. The
match was evidently approved by the lady's father,
for he proceeded to bestow on her as a dowry five
hundred acres of land on Manhattan Island, which
included the site of the present dwelling.

The year 1776 found the colonists in arms against the mother country, Roger Morris a colonel in the British army, and George Washington commander-in-chief of the forces of the colonies. Mrs. Morris occupied her home until the attack of the British on the city in August, 1776, when, finding that it was likely to become the theater of war, she left it hastily and found a refuge with the Tory people among the Highlands. A few days later General Washington arrived and made the house his headquarters during his operations on the island, holding stern councils of war in the drawing-room of the former mistress of his heart, and devoting to the repose of martial thews and sinews the downy beds and silken canopies that had been intended for far daintier uses. But this military occupation lasted only a short time, although the mistress of the mansion never returned to her charming retreat. At the close of the war her estates were confiscated, and she went with her husband to England, where she lived to a good old age.

Fourteen years later, in 1790, Washington, with a goodly number of dames and cavaliers, paid a second visit to the old dwelling. In his journal he has given us a detailed account of the event. He says, under date of July 10, 1790:

"Having formed a party consisting of the Vice-President, his lady, son and Miss Smith; the Secretaries of State, Treasury and War and the ladies of

THE RICHMOND HILL MANSION

Washington's Headquarters in 1776, and later the residence of John Adams and of Aaron Burr. Reproduced from a Valentine's Manual (1854) print in the collection of John D. Crimmins of New York

the two latter, with all the gentlemen of my family, Mrs. Lear and the two children, we visited the old position of Fort Washington, and afterward dined on a dinner provided by Mr. Mariner, at the house lately Colonel Roger Morris's, but confiscated and now in the possession of a common farmer."

This Captain Mariner was a noted character in the Revolution, and was engaged with Captain Hyler in the somewhat celebrated "whaleboat warfare," which consisted chiefly in making night descents on the enemy's coasts, and making prisoners of such prominent persons as came in their way. After the war he kept a tavern at Ward's Island and at Harlem, and became a noted caterer; it was in this capacity that he was employed to prepare the dinner for as imposing a company of guests as the mansion ever entertained.

In 1803 Morris's was again in the market, and for a time it seemed probable that Colonel Aaron Burr, who was then living in splendor at Richmond Hill would become its purchaser. In November of this year he wrote to his daughter Theodosia in regard to the exchange; her letter in reply, dated Clifton, S. C., December 10, 1803, is interesting as showing what one of the most charming and accomplished women of her day thought of the house. She says:

"The exchange has employed my thoughts ever since. Richmond Hill will, for a few years to come, be more valuable than Morris's, and to you, who are

so fond of town, a place so far from it would be use-
less; so much for my reasoning on one side; now for
the other.   Richmond Hill has lost many of its beauties
and is daily losing more.   If you mean it for a residence, what avails its intrinsic value ?   If you sell part
you deprive it of every beauty save the mere view.
Morris's has the most commanding view on the island;
it is reported to be indescribably beautiful.   The
grounds, too, are pretty; how many delightful walks
can be made on one hundred and thirty acres; how
much of your taste displayed!   In ten or twenty years
hence one hundred and thirty acres on New York
Island will be a principality; and there is to me something stylish, elegant, respectable and suitable to you
in having a handsome country seat.   So that, on the
whole, I vote for Morris's."

But Colonel Burr did not purchase the property at
this time, though thirty years later he married its
mistress, and resided there for some time, and met a
class of law students in the room formerly occupied
by Washington as his sleeping apartment.   The later
history of the mansion is both varied and interesting,
but is so near our own times that it is scarcely necessary to repeat it here.

An account of a visit which the writer made to it
recently, in company with a gentleman familiar not
only with the place but with its history as well, will
no doubt prove more acceptable.   The main hall,

which one enters from the pillared porch, is, with
its ancient portraits, its polished oaken floor and
great depth and roominess, the nearest approach
we have, perhaps, to that of an ancient baronial
castle. This hall opens by folding doors into the
drawing-room — the same that was used by Washington as a reception-room during his military
occupancy. Here he received his visitors, listened to
his orderlies' reports and dictated his answers, and
here at the last was held the council of war which
decided that Manhattan Island should be relinquished.
The floor of this room, and indeed of every apartment
in the house, is of oak, and so highly polished that it
affords an insecure footing to one used to carpeted
rooms. The wall paper has a groundwork of green,
with raised figures of vine and leaf having the appearance and texture of velvet, and its coloring is as fresh
and vivid as though nearly a century and a half had not
passed since it left the hand of the artisan. In this
room also hangs a beautiful chandelier, which was
formerly the property of the unfortunate French
General Moreau. A winding stairway at the right of
the hall leads the visitor to the suite of apartments
above, and ushers him first into a hall directly over the
one below, and of about the same dimensions. From
this hall one may step out upon a balcony which commands a magnificent view of city, river, and Sound.
Washington's bed-chamber was on this floor, at the

rear of the hall and directly over the drawing-room; there is nothing noteworthy about it except that it contains a number of secret doors and closets not all of which are known to the present residents. Two small ante-chambers, one on each side, were occupied by his aids, one of whom was Alexander Hamilton. The old oak bedstead on which Washington slept is still preserved with other treasured relics in the attic of the house.

Having seen all the objects of interest that the old house contained (although but a very few of them are included in this description) we were invited to a walk in the grounds, which are extensive, comprising about one hundred and thirty acres. Even here the antiquity of the place is apparent. The great locusts that line the main approach to the mansion are dead at the top and hoary with age. A great Madeira-nut tree, with gnarled trunk and wide-spreading branches, and a huge cedar of Lebanon, which was brought a tiny rootlet from its native mountain, could have been nourished to their present proportions only by a century of sun and showers; a hedge of slow-growing trees brought from Andalusia in Spain, which surrounds an ancient fountain's bed on the estate, also gives evidence of extreme age. After passing some time in the grounds and making pilgrimage to several points where charming views may be obtained, we took our leave, remarking on the striking contrast presented by

the old dwelling to the great city so near it, and speculating as to how long it can be protected from the
grasp of the giant which each day is bringing nearer
its gates.

CHAPTER IX

WE have a habit of observing each anniversary of the death of Washington Irving by a pilgrimage to Sleepy Hollow Cemetery, his last resting-place. It is but an hour to Tarrytown by rail from New York, and then a walk of a mile up the barrier hills to the sunny "Hollow," the bridge, and the churchyard. The conservatism of wealth and of tradition have united to preserve them as they were. Through the dell flows the silvery Pocantico issuing out of a deep glen to the eastward, and passing on under the arch of the old bridge forever famous as the scene of Ichabod Crane's nocturnal adventures. Near by is the little old Dutch church built of stone by the mighty patroon of Phillipburg half smothered in vines, with wooden belfry, and making weather cock and farm as uncanny as Alloway's Auld Haunted Kirk. In the shadow of its tower are the quaint, brown-stone tombs of the Van Warts, Van Tassels, and other famous families. The churchyard is as beautiful for situation as it is noteworthy in letters, being laid out on the western and southern slope of

the hill that rises steeply up from the Pocantico.   At
intervals on the hillside rocky crags protrude, veiled
by oak and hemlock, and in and out among these
curve the walks and drives.   The summit is occupied
by more modern memorials in marble and granite,
some quite tasteful and elaborate in design.   West of
these, perhaps half-way down the declivity, is the
Irving plot, characterized by a severe simplicity; it is
marked only by a low hedge of evergreens.   Its ten
or twelve tombstones are equally classic in their simplicity.   That of the author is on the south side of the
enclosure, and is a small, plain slab of marble, bearing
only his name, and the date of birth and death.   This
severe simplicity did not seem to us to be in good
taste; it was so incommensurate with the greatness of
the man, and the space he occupied in the literature
of his country, that it seemed incongruous.   It is, however, according to the sleeper's own request.   The
tomb is distinguished by one mark of public interest,
indicating that more than common dust sleeps beneath.   Each of its three faces has been chipped and
cut away by relic hunters, who have carried away the
fragments as souvenirs of their pilgrimage.

We could but contrast it with another American
shrine we had visited a few months previous [1]— the
tomb of Cooper in Cooperstown, just where the Susquehanna breaks from Otsego, its parent lake.   One can

[1] This article was written in 1885.

reach it from Richfield Springs by coach to the head
of the lake, and thence by steamer down its winding
shores, or he can drive over by private vehicle and not
consume a summer day. The village lies quiet and
peaceful in its deep cleft among the hills at the foot of
the lake. One easily finds the grave of the author in
the little Episcopal churchyard. It is almost in the
shadow of the sacred edifice, brooded over by somber
firs and pines, with the Susquehanna close by murmuring unceasing requiem! So strong a churchman
was Cooper, and attached to this little home church,
that I doubt if he could have rested quietly in stranger
ground. The novelist's grave is nearly in the center
of the plot, and that of the wife is beside her husband's;
both are marked by marble tablets resting on granite
pillars, and are without ornament save a simple cross
cut in the center of the stone. I had interest enough
to transcribe the inscription, as follows:

James Fenimore Cooper
born September 15th, 1789,
died September 14th, 1851.

Susan Augusta, wife of James Fenimore Cooper
and daughter of John Peter De Lancy
born January 28, 1792,
died January 20.

There is less popular appreciation of Cooper's tomb,
or is it that it is less accessible? it bears no marks of

the relic hunter's hammer, and the grass about it is
untrodden by pilgrim feet. Leaving the graves, we
strolled down the pleasant village street, in search of
the old Cooper Mansion, where the novelist lived
and in which much of his later work was done, but
learned that it had been burned to the ground some
thirty years before and its site made a waste. Some
strange fatality seems to attend American houses with
a history. The Hancock house in Boston, the tavern of
Israel Putnam in Brooklyn, Conn., the Franklin House
in Philadelphia, Webster's house at Green Harbor,
with scores of others that might be named have been
destroyed or so transformed that their interest and
identity are lost. Sunnyside, the home of Irving,
almost alone remains intact. The pilgrim to Sleepy
Hollow cannot better conclude his day than by a visit
thither. Leaving the churchyard one passes down the
main street of Tarrytown, lined with gray-stone castles
and elegant country-seats, quaint Dutch cottages and
modern villas, for two miles, and then enters a road
turning from it at right angles and leading down to
the Hudson. Soon one is lost in a maze of wildwood
greenery planted in a little gorge worn by a hillside
stream. Fine dwellings, with lawn and copse and
hedge, rustic bridges and parks of forest trees, are on
either side, and continue until one reaches a plateau
separated from the river only by the railroad tracks.
On this plateau, sheltered by fine old forest trees, stands

Sunnyside cottage. One realizes the felicity of its builder's description — "a quaint picturesque little pile." It is built of stone in ancient Dutch style, with crow-step gables and an L, and a multitude of nooks, crannies, and angles. The famous Melrose Abbey ivy, honeysuckle, rose vines and eglantines cover it in wildering mass. The main entrance is on the south, but there is a piazza on the west facing the river which, with its view of the broad Tappan Zee, the farther meadows of Tappan, and grim Palisades on the south, was the favorite resort of the author and his family in the long summer evenings. Though its clinging vines and antique style convey the impression of age, the cottage is comparatively modern, having been almost entirely remodeled in 1835. The old Dutch farmhouse which it originally was, is said to have been the Wolferts Roost, from which the partisan armed with his great goose gun stole out for his adventure with the marauders of the Tappan Zee. Later it came into the hands of the Van Tassels, and within its walls is said to have been held the merry-making from which Ichabod Crane departed for his terrible encounter with the Headless Horseman on the bridge by Sleepy Hollow Church.

Needless to add that the old house was the birthplace of those charming tales and sketches which have made the locality classic.

CHAPTER X

THE STORY OF THE PALATINES

THE period of American colonization was productive of many tragedies and romantic incidents,
few of which have been adequately sketched.

One of the most striking and least known of these
was the settlement in New York, in 1709, by the bounty
of Queen Anne of England, of a large body of Germans,
victims of religious persecution. The original home
of these interesting people was in what is known in
history as the Lower Palatinate of the Rhine, comprising two small states, which had been united previous
to 1620. It was a beautiful country of vineyards and
gardens, with a soft climate, under the mild government of an herediary ruler styled the Palatine. Prior
to the Reformation its people lived in the utmost
plenty and content. But their ruler early espoused
the cause of Luther, and, in the fierce religious wars
that followed, the Palatinate was in many instances
the battle-ground of the contending parties. Yet the
people recovered quickly from every blow, and still
clung to their land and faith. At length, in 1689, the
armies of Louis XIV of France marched into the

country and ravaged it utterly, the pretext being that
it was used as a haven of refuge for the king's Huguenot
subjects, whom he was then engaged in extirpating.
Everything was utterly destroyed except the bare soil,
— churches, houses, public buildings, cattle, fair fields,
pleasant vineyards. In that time of terror the Elector
from his castle at Mannheim beheld two cities and
twenty-five towns in flames. Lust and cruelty were
satiated. The people pleading for mercy on bended
knees were thrust forth into the fields. Three thousand one hundred and fifty square miles of territory
were left a blackened waste, and the wretched inhabitants driven into exile. Wandering homeless and
friendless through Europe for several years, the thoughts
of the more intelligent among them turned at length
to England as a possible haven. Good Queen Anne
had succeeded to the English throne: ties of blood connected her with the hapless Count Palatine, she being
a cousin of the first degree: besides, she was known to
sympathize deeply with the persecuted Protestants of
Europe, of every nationality. And so it happened
that in the spring of 1708 a little band of Palatine
exiles landed at Whitehall and filed through the London streets in search of friends among their co-religionists. There were forty-one of them, — men, women,
and children, — natives of Neuberg on the Rhine, and
all bore certificates of good character and that they
had been stripped of everything by the army of France,

signed by the bailiffs of their native town. Their leader was a grave, thoughtful man of mature years, — their pastor, Joshua Kockerthal, "Evangelical minister," as he is called in the Lords of Trade Documents, — a Great-heart who had led the little band in all their wanderings and had now safely conducted them to England. Pastor Kockerthal lost no time in presenting to Queen Anne a petition, in which he asked to be sent with his own company, and others of his countrymen that might follow, to her majesty's colonies in America.

Never did petition receive from authority a more favorable hearing. Queen Anne's womanly heart was moved to pity by the woes of the exiles. To her ministers the petition seemed to open the way to a master-stroke of policy in the settlement of the colonies. The aggressions of the French in Canada were then beginning to be felt along the whole northern frontiers of New England and New York, and the planting of a large body of Germans, natural enemies of France, on the frontier was a policy to be pursued with spirit. They heartily seconded, therefore, the queen's design of sending the petitioners to her colony of New York. The queen defrayed the cost of their transit, it is said, from her own private purse. Sending for Pastor Kockerthal, she questioned him concerning his history and that of his people, promised him free transportation with his company to their new homes, and agreed further to furnish them with seed, agricultural tools, and furniture, lands free of tax and quit-rent, and to support them for one year, or until their first harvest could be reaped. To Pastor Kockerthal Queen Anne was even more generous, granting him five hundred acres as a glebe for the support of his wife and children besides a *douceur* of twenty pounds for the purchase of books and clothing. The males were also naturalized by the Crown before leaving. The ship Lyon was got ready, and sailed early in August, 1708, in company with Lord Lovelace, who had been appointed governor of New York. There were fifty-two Palatines on board, — one a babe of two weeks, and several others of tender age.

The majority of the adults were vinedressers and husbandmen; but there were also a smith, a carpenter, a weaver, and a stocking-maker among them. Few particulars of the voyage have been preserved. They had a long and stormy passage of more than four months, reaching New York late in December, 1708. Several of the passengers had died on the voyage, nearly all were sick, and the whole company was quarantined for some weeks on Staten Island before being admitted to the city. As soon as possible, Lord Lovelace set about selecting a site for their settlement. On the west bank of the Hudson, just above the Highlands, familiar now to travelers as the site of the city of Newburgh, there was a tract of country that in soil and natural scenery was thought as near an approach to that of the Rhine as could be found in the New World; and here the little band of storm-tossed voyagers was established.

The tract granted them comprised two thousand one hundred and ninety acres, and was laid out in nine lots leading back from the river, including a glebe of five hundred acres for the minister. Here the wanderers made a clearing, erected houses, built roads and bridges, and, in due time, added a church and school-house, which Queen Anne furnished with a bell,[1] and thus laid the foundations of an enterprising and flourishing town.

Pastor Kockerthal remained only long enough to establish his flock in their fold. The country pleased him. The government had fulfilled its promises to

[1] This bell is still preserved in the city of Newburgh as a precious relic. It is a small bell, of about twenty-five pounds' weight, very sweet in tone, and bears the inscription "*Una fecit Amsterdammi,* 17—." Its vicissitudes have been many. When first given to the Palatines, their church was not ready, and it was loaned for a season to the Lutheran church in New York. On the abdication of their grant by the Palatines, it became the property of the Church of England, which succeeded to the glebe, and on the outbreak of the Revolution was buried in a swamp to prevent its falling into the hands of the Whigs. Later it called the village children to school and then, in a few years superseded in this high office by a new bell, it was hung in the stables of the village hotel to give the hour to the workmen. When the writer first saw it, in the spring of 1882, it hung in a grocery-store; and he understands that it has since been removed to the Washington Head quarters for preservation.

the letter, and he felt that he could not remain at ease
until his bruised and smitten countrymen in Germany
had been brought to this land of plenty and liberty.
In a few months he embarked, again made the tem-
pestuous voyage, appeared before the queen, and,
having gained her countenance for his project, set out
for Germany to collect his co-religionists and lead
them, a second Joshua, to the promised land. By the
fall of 1709 he had assembled three thousand exiles
at different points on the Rhine, eager for the enterprise, and late in the year they came to England,
touching on the way at Leyden.

The English government had encouraged Pastor
Kockerthal's mission, if it had not directly authorized
it: still, with a lynx-eyed opposition scanning its every
move, it hesitated at incurring the expense of trans-
porting this large body of emigrants to America and
subsisting them there for a twelvemonth, as it had
done their predecessors. There happened to be in
London at this juncture a gentleman — Colonel
Robert Hunter — who, having been recently appointed
governor of New York, took a great interest in the
affairs of the province, and who suggested a plan for
relieving the ministry of its difficulty. This plan was
to employ the Palatines after their arrival in the production of naval stores until the expenses of their
transit had been fully met. In 1698 a commission had
been appointed to inquire into the capacity of the

American colonies for the production of naval stores, and to survey the woods and forests for masts, oak timber, pitch-pine, and land suitable for the production of hemp, the sanguine ministers evidently believing that American oak in English shipyards was something to be desired. A bounty had also been offered for every barrel of tar or turpentine imported from America. Colonel Hunter's reasonings on the subject, as subsequently adopted and reported by the Lords of Trade to the queen, were novel and interesting. "Your majesty," it was argued, "imports four thousand seven hundred barrels of tar yearly from the Baltic States. It has been found in America that one man can make six tons of stores per year; and several working together could make double that in proportion. We suppose that six hundred men employed in it will produce seven thousand tons a year, which, if more than your majesty needs, could be profitably employed in trade with Spain and Portugal." The cost of production was estimated at five pounds a ton, and that of transportation at four pounds, at which figures it could be sold as low as Norway tar; and calculations were made to show how easy it would be in this way for the Palatines to refund the money advanced them, while at the same time they could be making their homes in the wilderness. The recommendations of the Lords of Trade were adopted.

The Palatines signed a contract agreeing to settle

on such lands as should be allotted them, not to leave them without the governor's permission, not to engage in woolen-manufacture, and to suffer the naval stores produced to be devoted to the payment of the money advanced. The queen, on her part, agreed to transport them to New York, to subsist them for one year after their arrival, to furnish them with seed and implements, and to grant them, *as soon as the debt was paid*, forty acres of land each, to be free of tax or quit-rent for seven years. There was at this time in the beautiful Mohawk Valley, on the site of the present towns of Herkimer and German Flats, a tract of ungranted land to which the Indians held a quasi claim, although it was not occupied by them; and this was selected as the site of the Palatine settlement.

To Colonel Hunter was assigned the duty of planting the exiles in their new home. The instructions given to this gentleman show that much machinery was set in motion by the enterprise. Mr. Bridger, her majesty's Surveyor-General of America, was ordered down from New England to instruct the people in the art of making tar. Overseers were appointed to keep them at work, at a salary of one hundred pounds per annum, a commissary to receive the stores, at two hundred pounds for himself and clerk, and a factor in England to place the stores on the market there, at the usual rate of commission. Ten vessels were

got ready to transport the colony.   They rendezvoused
at Plymouth, the point of departure of so many pilgrim
companies, and here, early in the spring of 1710, the
company embarked.   The scene must have been one
of unusual and pathetic interest, though no account
of it has come down to us.   The voyage was to be the
complement of twenty years' wanderings, and its end
rest, competency, home.   So large an hegira had never
been known before, at least in modern times, and was
not subsequently equaled.   Three thousand people,
— men, women, children, babes in arms, — representing nearly all crafts, professions, and conditions,
gathered on the pier, all placed on a level by one hard
condition, — biting poverty.   There were hand-shak-
ings and mutual farewells, then the heave-ho of the
sailors, the filling of sails, and the fleet moved slowly
out of the harbor.   Tradition says that an event of
evil moment attended the departure: a boat passing
from one ship to another was capsized and all its passengers drowned; and almost before the land had sunk
from view a storm arose and scattered the fleet, one
vessel — the Berkeley Castle — being so disabled that
she was obliged to put into Portsmouth for repairs,
and reached New York several days behind the other
vessels.   The voyage was long and disastrous.   Crowded
into small vessels, supplied probably with insufficient
food, tossed by the sea, and worn out by their previous sufferings, sickness broke out among the poor

people, and death reaped a fearful harvest. Almost
the only details of the passage are given in two letters
from Governor Hunter to the Lords of Trade, dated
at New York, — the first, June 16, 1710, in which he
says that he had arrived there two days before, and
adds, "We want three of the Palatine ships, and those
arrived are in a desperately sickly condition." He
writes again July 24, "The Palatine ships are all safe,
except the Herbert frigate, with tents and arms, cast
away on the east end of Long Island, July 7. The
men are safe, the goods damaged. The Berkeley
Castle, left at Portsmouth, not in. The poor people
have been mighty sickly, but recover apace. We have
lost about four hundred and seventy of our number."
Four hundred and seventy out of a total of three
thousand!

The exiles once landed, Mr. Bridger was sent off
to the Mohawk lands to see if they were suited for the
purpose in view, and returned in due time with an un-
favorable report. The lands were undoubtedly good,
he admitted, but the entire absence of pines precluded
the idea of using them for the production of naval
stores; and even if pines were to be had, their remote-
ness from market was an insuperable objection : besides,
if the people were settled on these extreme frontiers
they could not be protected from the inroads of the
French and Indians, — as if the government had not
designed planting them there as a check to those in-

roads. To get a correct idea of the animus of this report, we must glance briefly at the state of the colony of New York. After the conquest of India, it came to be regarded as an asylum for bankrupt politicians and impecunious younger sons of the English nobility, who went out poor, and in a few years, by the simple process of peculation in office, returned rich. New York at this time sustained much such a relation to the mother country, though of course in lesser degree. Pirates and smugglers in the ports, land-grabbers, tax-collectors, and commissaries in the interior, offered rare opportunities to officials with itching palms. Most of the land then taken up was held in great estates by certain patroons and lords of manors, who held the rights of the commonalty in utter contempt. These men had great influence with the colonial government. There was what would be called now a "ring" at Albany, that had already cast covetous eyes on the beautiful Mohawk Valley and were not willing that it should be given to a band of needy German emigrants.

While Mr. Bridger was making his survey, Governor Hunter had been approached on the subject by one of these gentlemen, Robert Livingston. Mr. Livingston was a native of Scotland, a man of ability and great force of character, who, in several offices had done the colony good service, but who was tainted with the leprosy of covetousness. By means of these offices and his interest with the royal governors he had become very wealthy, and was now the owner of a manor of one hundred and sixty thousand acres. His manor-house stood some six miles back from the Hudson, on a knoll overlooking one of the intervales of the river, and has been described as "a long, low, rambling dwelling of stone, with heavy roofs, stout oaken doors, and windows so deeply set in the walls that they looked like embrasures." Within it was furnished with some approach to European elegance. Over his wide domain Livingston ruled as an autocrat. He had been endowed with all the rights enjoyed by English lords of the manor, had many retainers in his hall, many horses in his stalls, and the command of a militia company formed of his followers, all of which combined with his free hospitality to make him popular at home and potent in affairs of state.

Mr. Livingston advanced the objections to the Mohawk lands which have been stated, and proposed instead a tract of six thousand acres on his own manor, heavily timbered, contiguous to the river, and in every way suited to the object. He would dispose of it for such a purpose at a sacrifice, — four hundred pounds sterling. Without entering into details, we may say that the offer was accepted. In October, 1710, the poor Palatines, robbed of the Canaan which had been promised them, were planted in the gloomy pine forest on the Livingston estate. Some refused the hard conditions and remained in New York, founding there the first Lutheran church in this country; others joined their countrymen in Pennsylvania. Those that went were settled in five villages, or " dorfs," — three on the east bank, known as the East Camp, and two on the west bank, directly opposite, on a tract of un-granted land, called West Camp. Two thousand two hundred and twenty-seven Palatines were settled here, the remainder having died or been left at New York and other points.

Queen Anne, it will be remembered, had agreed to maintain the colonists for a year after their arrival. The stated daily stipend had been fixed at sixpence for adults and fourpence for children before leaving England. The contract for supplying them was given to Livingston. The rations furnished, according to the terms of his contract, which is still in existence, were a third of a loaf of bread a day, the loaves of such size and sort as were sold in New York for fourpence halfpenny, and a quart of beer from his brew-house. The first act of the settlers was to build rude log houses for shelter; their next, to clear the ground. The homes so long and ardently looked forward to were at last theirs. How depressingly must they have compared with the homes they had left! Instead of the smiling fields and vineyards of the Fatherland, a gloomy pine forest, extending far as the eye could reach; instead of the Rhine, a sullen, forest-fringed river; in place of busy city and romantically-perched castle, the log hut of the settler and the wigwam of the savage. Quite different, too, from what they had been accustomed to were the duties that awaited them here. Instead of the reaping and sowing, dressing of the vine and treading of the purple vintage, the hard, thankless task of the pioneer, — forests to hew, houses to build, lands to clear, roads to open, a dock to construct; and to these was added the drudgery of a distasteful occupation. The first winter they were employed in building houses and making clearings. In the spring, under harsh taskmasters, they began discharging their obligations to the queen, and continued it, many of them, for twelve long years of servitude.

Their first act was to prepare the trees for tar-making. In the spring, when the sap was up, they barked the north side of the tree; in the fall, before the sap was down, the south side; in the succeeding spring, the east side, and in the fall again, the west side, — the object being to retain the sap in the wood. Two years were required by this process to prepare the tree. Then, when it was fully dead, it was cut into convenient lengths, and the tar extracted from it by slow combustion in a rude kiln. Turpentine was extracted by bleeding the trees, as is now practised. So earnest were the overseers that the boys and girls were set to gathering pine knots, from which alone, Governor Hunter reported, sixty barrels of tar were made during the first season.

It was not long before the poor Palatines discovered that they had sold themselves into a virtual slavery. The clause in their contract which granted them their lands only when they should have repaid the cost of their transportation was fatal to their liberty; for it soon became apparent that naval stores could not be produced on the Hudson so cheaply and of such quality as the British ministry had predicted, that when sold in open market they could not compete with the Swedish article, and that after the salaries of instructors, commissaries, overseers, agents, and clerks were paid, very little was left to the credit of the Palatines. The prospect of discharging their debt by these means in that century seemed hopeless. The condition of the emigrants soon became pitiable: they were looked upon as paupers subsisting on the bounty of government, and treated accordingly. The neighboring white settlers regarded them as interlopers, and had little intercourse with them, and then only to fan their discontent. Nearly all the officials made a spoil of them; but none aroused so many bitter complaints as did the chief commissary, Robert Livingston. It was alleged that the bread he furnished them was moldy and lacked the stipulated weight, and that the beer was so bad as to be undrinkable; furthermore, that by his interest with the overseers they were oftener employed in clearing the manor lands than on their own reser-

vation.[1] More than once these complaints became so
bitter that Governor Hunter came in person to in-
vestigate them. He was accompained by his staff,
and was received with every mark of consideration
and respect at the manor-house. Samples of the
bread and beer furnished were shown him; he heard
the statements of the contractor; and the conclusion
of the matter was a speech to the disaffected, in which
he recounted the goodness of the queen and upbraided
them for a set of sturdy rogues who were making but
a poor return for the favors shown them.

They had, however, other grounds of complaint.
Sickness was rife among them, and they were without
medicines or physicians. Their children were bound

---

[1] A caustic letter from the Earl of Clarendon to Lord Dartmouth,
Secretary of State, gives color to these charges. He says: "I think
it unhappy that Colonel Hunter at his first arrival in his government
has fallen into such ill hands, for this Livingston has been known
many years in that province for a very ill man. He formerly vict-
ualled the forces at Albany, in which he was guilty of most notorious
frauds by which he greatly improved his estate. He has a mill and
brew-house upon his land, and if he can get the victualling of the
Palatines, who are so conveniently posted for his purpose, he will make
a good addition to his estate. . . . I am of opinion, if subsistence
be all, the conclusion will be that Livingston and some others will
get large estates, the Palatines will be none the richer, but will be
confirmed in that laziness they are already prone to." The earl,
however, was opposed to the emigration of the Palatines. It is just
to Livingston to say that a commissioner appointed to inquire into
his accounts while quartermaster exonerated him from charges
of fraud.

out without their consent, and, under colonial law, became the property of their masters as absolutely as the cattle in their stalls. In 1711, in the war against Canada, a requisition for soldiers had been served upon them, and three hundred of their best men had accompanied Colonel Nicholson in the campaign against Montreal, — not all of whom returned. Their chief grievance, however, lay in the fact that the beautiful country which had been promised them, and which was to furnish homes for themselves and their children, was withheld, — that by a clause in the contract which they had misunderstood they were held in bondage. There was much discontent among them on these grounds during the first winter, not allayed when some bold spirits who had penetrated the wilderness to the promised land returned with glowing accounts of its beauty and fertility.

Good Pastor Kockerthal spent most of his time with his afflicted brethren, leaving the little flock at Newburgh to the care of local elders. He attended the sick, and knelt at the bedside of the dying with prayers and words of consolation. He counseled patience and moderation, cheered them with the hymns of the Fatherland, and was until death the guide and comforter of the people.[1]

[1] This unsung apostle died in 1719, and was buried in the midst of the people he had loved so well. His grave is still to be seen in West Camp, in the present town of Saugerties, — a sort of vault

The pastor was powerless to allay all feeling of discontent, however, and in May, 1711, Governor Hunter was hastily summoned to the manor to quell a mutiny which had broken out among the Palatines. They had risen against their overseers, he was told, declaring that they would go to the lands at Schoharie which the queen had given them. Hunter, with sixty soldiers whom he had ordered down from the garrison at Albany, marched into the midst of the villages and summoned the chiefs to an account. They stated their grievances, which have been enumerated.

The governor, in reply, reminded them of their solemn contract, and of their obligations to the queen, assured them that the Scoharie country was still

in a field near the Hudson, covered with a large flat stone, on which is inscribed, in German, this mystical epitaph:

Wise Wanderer
Under this stone rests near his
Sybilla Charlotte
A True Wanderer
The Joshua
of the High Dutch in North America and the
same in the East and West
Hudson's River
Poor Lutheran Preacher
His first arrival was with Lord Lovelace 1707–8
January the 1st
His second was with Col. Hunter 1710
June the 14th
His voyage to England brought forth his heavenly
voyage on St. John's Day 1719.

occupied by Indians, and that if they were settled there they could not be protected from the French. They still continued rebellious, however, and he ended the matter summarily by disarming them and putting them under the care of captains or directors, as the queen's hired servants. After this exploit he returned to New York. For a year the Palatines, deprived of their arms and under the eye of the military, remained passive.

Pastor Kockerthal, writing of them at this period, says: "All are at work and busy, but manifestly with repugnance and only temporarily. They think the tract intended for them a Canaan, but dangerous to settle now, so they have patience. But they will not listen to tar-making." In the fall of 1712 the governor informed them that they must depend upon themselves for subsistence thereafter, as his funds were exhausted. The winter passed in not very successful efforts to keep the wolf from the door, and in laying plans for a removal to Scoharie as soon as spring should open. This region seems to have been the Canaan of the wanderers. Roseate visions of it had been flitting through their minds since their departure from England. Hunters and trappers with whom they came in contact gave glowing accounts of its beauty and fertility. It lay in the valley of the Scoharie, near its junction with the Mohawk, some thirty miles west of Albany. It was a natural prairie of rich, deep soil,

once used by the Indians for corn-lands, but which
in their retreat westward had been abandoned.

Early in May, 1713, a large body of the people,
some five hundred in number, proceeded by water to
Albany, with the purpose of entering the valley from
thence. Conrad Weiser, one of the seven captains,
was the leader, — Pastor Kockerthal remaining at the
Camps. There is no more beautiful drive to-day
than the old road from Albany to Scoharie, which
follows the line of the Indian trail that led the emigrants
to their happy valley. The company journeyed on
foot: they had neither vehicle nor draft-animal of
any sort. The men carried their arms, seeds, implements, and household effects on their backs; each
matron had a babe in arms, a group of little toddlers
beside her, and perhaps a sack of provisions or bundle
of clothing on her back. An Indian, in paint and
feathers, led the way. Thus accoutered, they were
three days making the journey. At night they camped
in the open air, building fires to keep away the wolves.
Up the heights of the Helderberg, one of the northern-
most spurs of the Catskills, they toiled, and on over
ridge and valley, until, on the third day, from the
foot-hills of Fox Creek they caught sight of the Schoharie intervale. It is dotted now with villages and
rich with broad, green fields surrounding farmhouses
where content and abundance reside, — one of the
garden-spots of the Empire State, — a valley so lovely

that when viewed on a June day from its encircling hills the eye is loath to turn from the entrancing sight. It was beautiful then, though art had done nothing for it; and eagerly the wanderers thronged into it and began the erection of their homes. They established themselves in seven villages, each named after its head man, and to each householder was allotted forty acres of land to clear, fence, and till as his own. The settlement soon grew into a thrifty and prosperous community, and for sixty years nothing occurred to disturb its serenity except the recurrence of one question, that of the title to the lands.

At an early period, Nicholas Bayard, an agent of the Crown, arrived, and sent word to the householders that if they would describe to him the boundaries of their land he would give them a free deed in the name of the queen. But the people had grown suspicious of government officials, and, looking on this as some new device to deprive them of their lands, treated the agent so roughly that he fled to Schenectady. From that place he again offered to give to whoever would appear there with a single car of corn and describe his boundaries a free deed and title in perpetuity. The people, however, still suspicious, refused this offer; and Bayard then repaired to Albany, where he sold the title to the Scoharie lands to five landholders, — one of them being Robert Livingston, Jr. These gentlemen soon called on the settlers, either to purchase the lands they had cleared, take out loans, or be evicted, and, no notice being taken of the summons, sent the sheriff of Albany to dispossess them. It was a general notion that the Palatines were a mild, inoffensive, pusillanimous people, who would submit to any injustice rather than break the peace: so the sheriff proceeded on his mission unaccompanied by even a deputy, and, putting up at the public house in Weiser's dorf, made known his conditions to the villagers. It is not recorded that the men made any objection to these harsh terms; but the mob of women that soon gathered at the door convinced him that he had made a mistake. They were Amazons, these women, strong daughters of the hoe and plough, bare-armed, scant of skirt, strong-limbed from frequent journeys to Schenectady bearing the bag of grain to be floured; and it was but the work of a moment for two of them to hustle the little sheriff from his retreat into their midst. There he was knocked down, rolled in the mire where the hogs wallowed, and then placed on a rail and ridden "skimmington" through four villages, — Hartman's, Bruna's, Smith's, and Fox's dorfs, — in all, hissed and hooted at and pelted with mud as the rogue who had come to deprive the people of their homes. At length the poor wretch, more dead than alive, was set down on the Mill bridge, seven miles from his starting-point, and bidden to betake himself to his masters, lest worse evils should befall him. Our heroines, however, paid dearly for their sport on this occasion. For a long time their liege-lords refused to go to Albany to trade, sending their wives instead, well knowing that they would be held responsible for the sheriff's discomfiture. After a while, however, thinking the storm had blown over, several of them ventured, and were summarily seized by the proprietors and kept in prison until they agreed to pay the price demanded for their lands.

It is time, however, that we should return to glance briefly at the history of their fellow-pioneers whom we left on the Hudson. These as a body remained where Governor Hunter had placed them until after the death of the good pastor Kockerthal in 1719. In 1721 some of the more enterprising began agitating a removal to the rich bottomlands of the Mohawk promised by Queen Anne. Their agents were sent out, and selected a tract of land at the confluence of Canada Creek with the Mohawk, on which the prosperous towns of Herkimer and German Flats now stand. Governor Burnett confirmed this tract to them by a patent dated January 17, 1722, and a detachment of ninety-two persons made a settlement here, probably in the spring of that year. To each head of a family was allotted forty acres of land, and the industry of the owners soon made every acre as productive as a garden.

The long-coveted material for homes was at last

secured to them, and hope made every muscle active
and enduring. For thirty-five years the settlers lived
a sort of Acadian life. Their Indian neighbors, the
Six Nations, through the influence of Sir William
Johnson, continued at peace with the English. Questions of title and boundaries which disturbed their
compatriots at Scoharie were never raised here.
Their lands were perhaps the richest ever tilled, and,
with their simple and economical habits, a generation
was sufficient to make them thrifty and comfortable
land-holders, with large framed dwellings, capacious
barns, schools, churches, and mills. This fair dream
of peace was rudely dispelled, however, in the autumn
of 1757, when a body of three hundred French and
Indians, under M. De Belêtre, suddenly appeared
before the settlements on the north side of the Mohawk.
Part of the inhabitants fled to rude forts, or, rather,
block-houses, which had been constructed for such an
emergency, and from this retreat beheld the torch
applied to their houses, barns, and ricks, their live-
stock herded for driving away, and such of their relatives as had not been able to reach the fort captured
or inhumanly butchered. Next the enemy appeared
before the block-house and summoned the people to
surrender, threatening to show no mercy if compelled
to take it, and the captains, deeming discretion the
better part of valor, opened the gates. The commanding officer then massed the prisoners, as he had the

plunder, and the long, weary march to Canada was
begun. The settlement was utterly laid waste. Sixty
buildings were burned, forty dead were left on the
ground unburied, and one hundred and fifty men,
women, and children were borne away into the wilderness to suffer the horrors of Indian captivity.

The settlements on the south side, directly opposite,
were untouched, the ravagers fearing to remain long
in the neighborhood, lest news of their exploits should
bring Sir Willaim and his Iroquois upon them. With
this single exception, however, the three principal
Palatine settlements — on the Mohawk, the Scoharie, and the Hudson — enjoyed, during the colonial
era, the blessings of peace. Sir William died early in
1774, some said by his own hand to avoid acting against
his friends in the struggle which he saw to be inevitable.
The struggle quickly followed his death, and it found
the unhappy Palatines on the border between the two
contending factions. Fate to this people must have
seemed inexorable. Considering the persecutions and
miseries they had suffered in the Old World, the oppres-
sions and extortions that met them in the New, and
the horrors visited upon them in the Revolutionary
struggle, we must admit that there never lived a people
more hardly used. At the beginning of hostilities, it
will be remembered, the Six Nations renewed their
allegiance to the British cause, and the Crown at once
let them loose on the American settlements, stimulating

their native ferocity by the offer of a bounty of eight dollars for every scalp brought in.

The Palatine settlements, from their defenseless condition, and the fact that the people were less skilful in the use of arms than their Yankee neighbors, became early a favorite hunting-ground for the red rangers. The murders, burnings, torturings, and other atrocities committed here during the war would be deemed incredible were they not so well authenticated. Wives saw their husbands murdered, scalped, and impaled on the pickets that fenced their gardens. Wives were brained and scalped before the eyes of their husbands, children in the presence of their parents; babes were torn from their mothers' breasts to be dashed upon the stones; and the hellish carnival generally ended with the burning of all that the settler had gathered by years of toil, and the carrying away into captivity of such as savage fancy had spared.

These outrages were committed, not by large bodies of men whose coming could be discovered and guarded against, but by detached bands, whose approach was as stealthy as the panther's and who sprang upon the settlements in the secure hour when no danger was apprehended. Their effect was to almost depopulate the Mohawk Valley. In 1781 it was estimated that fully one third of the inhabitants had been killed or captured; and most of the remainder had fled within the American lines for safety.

It is pleasant to know, however, that this was the last severe affliction visited upon this long-suffering people. After the war the survivors returned to their ruined homes; the soil was left them, and returned generous harvests, as if in pity for their misfortunes, and a generation later the visitor to the beautiful valley could discover scarcely a trace of the ruthless hand of war.

CHAPTER XI

LOITERING at Ticonderoga, through bright autumn days, long after the stream of tourists had run away, we made many voyages of discovery, each so interesting that it might with profit occupy a week of a summer sojourn. One should establish himself at the pretty village of Ticonderoga, up the outlet of Lake George, where one finds good hotels and all the amenities. Lake George is three miles away on the south, and Lake Champlain two miles on the east, while at the door in the falls of the outlet is almost every variety of form that falling water can assume. This outlet, as it leaves Lake George, is a considerable mill stream of clear cold water, sparkling and murmuring among meadows until reaching the village it falls nearly 250 feet in as many yards, covering almost at a leap the difference in level between the two lakes. In its natural state the cataract must have been a romantic picture, but its waters are now [1] so obstructed by dams and vexed by mill-wheels that much of their beauty has vanished. Pulp mills en-

[1] This was written in 1886.

RUINS OF FORT TICONDEROGA, LAKE CHAMPLAIN
Reproduced from an old print. The ruins are on the lower hill at the right

gaged in making paper from the poplar which grows
along the lake shore, a woolen mill, and long, low
workshops, in which the graphite found in the neighboring hills is prepared for market, are now clustered
beside the cataract, and about them lies the village
comprising some 1900 inhabitants. Below, the outlet flows through a woody glen to Lake Champlain,
so deep and quiet that it is easily navigable by small
steamers; and then comes the lake, — so narrow and
shallow here that the Vermont Central has thrown a
draw-bridge across it to connect its system with that
of the Delaware and Hudson, but lengthening itself
out like a ribbon to Whitehall, twenty-two miles south.
One might spend days rounding the fir-clad promon-
tories or skirting the gently-circling bay shores without discovering one half its beauties.

The great feature of interest, however, is old Fort
Ticonderoga. As one glides from the outlet into the
lake he sees over a marsh on the left a gaunt, craggy
promontory rising abruptly out of the water and
stretching back into the forest a well-defined wall of
trap a hundred feet above the level of the lake. The
railway coming up from Whitehall pierces the barrier
by a tunnel. On the right, in the curve of the bay
formed partly by this promontory, is the dock where
the large lake steamers land their passengers for Lake
George. This promontory is Ticonderoga, one of the
most historic spots in America. Clambering up its

ledges to the summit, one finds a green, slightly rolling plateau, with black rocks outcropping here and there among the grass, and in its center gaunt and ragged walls of masonry. In some of them embrasures still gape, and beside them moat and sally-port, north and west bastions, parade, and barracks are still traceable. A little further east, where the cliff projects over the water, may be defined the outlines of a redoubt. Sheep are feeding now among the grim ruins, and one may linger all day without being disturbed by any chance passer. It is a strange, eventful history that of this rock. When the French engineers of Baron Dieskau first selected it, and raised here the walls of their Fort Carillon, they did it to command the great highway between the English colonies on the south and their own Dominion of Canada, a highway which, making use of the Hudson and the two lakes — George and Champlain — gave almost uninterrupted water communication between the St. Lawrence and the Atlantic at New York. And so it came about that all the wars between these French and English colonies resolved themselves into a struggle for the possession of this commanding rock. In like manner it became the first point aimed at and won by the American colonies in their later struggle against England for independence. Strange memories cluster about the gray old ruin, which a dreamy October day is apt to revivify. First a thousand gay Frenchmen in blue coats, and half as many Iroquois in war paint and feathers, march away up the outlet toward Lake George, bound on the congenial errand of a midnight assault on some unguarded fortress or sleeping settlement. But in a few days they come streaming back broken, defeated. They have met Johnson and his provincials at Fort William Henry, at the head of the lake. Next, Vaudreuil comes on the same errand, wading through the March snows, but is broken on the same sturdy barrier. But the Frenchmen still persist, and five months later Montcalm, with pennons waving over 8000 men in arms, comes up the lake bound to sweep the English from Lake George. He does it, but the year is hardly out ere Abercrombie, with 15,000 Englishmen, sits down before the fort and demands its surrender. There is a heady fight, and the fort holds out, but the English retreat only to reappear the next year under an abler general, and overthrow the French power in America.

Under English rule the old fort saw peaceful days. The quiet lakes were no more the field of contending nations. Iroquois and Mohawks went no more on the warpath. A corporal's guard of forty men lounged about the crumbling ramparts, watched the lizard basking in the sally-port, drank King George's health, and shuffled cards on unused drumheads. Then came the morning of the 10th of May, 1775, when in the gray dawn a motley band of frontiersmen in backwoods garb, headed by one Ethan Allen, of Bennington, swarmed over the parapets and drew up on the parade. We should like to have seen the expression of the old red-faced martinet who commanded when confronted by this band of farmers and ordered to surrender "in the name of the great Jehovah and the Continental Congress."

CHAPTER XII

GLIDING swiftly eastward on the New York Central Railroad and nearing the little village of Oriskany, in Oneida County, a tall shaft on a neighboring hilltop to the right flashed by. The monument is to General Herkimer and the brave patriots of 1777, and it marks the Oriskany battle-field as well. The whole region is storied ground. We left the train at the little station of Oriskany, and walked back along the tow-path of the canal for the first mile, thence across the latter by a bridge and along a rural lane to the highway which skirts the brow of the hill on which the monument stands. In his cottage overlooking the battle-field, we found Mr. Rolin M. Lewis, the custodian of the grounds, who added much to the interest of our visit by personally guiding us to the scenes of greatest interest, and which, being unmarked, we would have found by ourselves difficult to determine.

The monument stands where the battle was fought, on the edge of a sharp bluff rearing itself above the Mohawk Valley, on a plot of five acres of meadow purchased by the Association for the purpose. It is of Maine granite, eighty-five feet high above the base, which is of the valley limestone. On each side of the die of the pedestal is a tablet of bronze six feet wide and four and a half high. Two of the bronzes are pictorial, and represent one, General Herkimer directing the fight after receiving his mortal wound, the other a pioneer and Indian engaged in deadly struggle. On one of the remaining tablets is the dedication, and on the other a roster containing the names of those patriots engaged in the fight, as far as they could be learned — but 250 out of 800. The dedication was written by Professor Edward North, of Hamilton College, and is in excellent taste. It is as follows:

"Here was fought the battle of Oriskany on the 6th day of August, 1777. Here British invasion was checked and thwarted. Here Gen. Nicholas Herkimer, intrepid leader of the American forces, though mortally wounded, kept command of the fight, till the enemy had fled. The life blood of more than 200 patriot heroes made this battle-ground sacred forever.

"This Monument was built A.D. 1883 in the year of Independence 107, by grateful dwellers in the Mohawk Valley, under the direction of the Oneida Historical Society, aided by the National Government and the State of New York."

THE ORISKANY MONUMENT

The first mover in the matter of erecting this monument was the Continental Congress of 1777, which passed the following resolution:

"That the Governor and Council of New York be desired to erect a monument at Continental expense of the value of $500 to the memory of the late Brigadier-General Herkimer, who commanded the militia of Tryon County, in the State of New York, and was killed fighting gallantly in defence of the liberties of these States."

But the people were too poor to give effect to this praiseworthy resolution, and it slumbered until in 1876 the Oneida Historical Society was formed at Utica, when it actively began the work so long delayed. Public meetings were held, the press enlisted, Congress was appealed to, and at length induced to vote the original sum of $500, with interest amounting to $4100, to which the Legislature of New York added $3000 conditional to a like sum being raised by private subscription. The monument was erected in 1883, and dedicated with appropriate ceremonies, in the presence of a large audience, on the 6th of August, 1884, the 107th anniversary of the battle.

The visitor can but be charmed with the outlook from the spot. At his feet is the winding, gently undulating valley of the Upper Mohawk, covered with tilth and grange, the new-born river sparkling in its midst. The Erie Canal runs at the foot of the bluff, and beside it the great national highway, the New York Central, with its four roadways over which ten trains every hour pass. Half-a-dozen boats are in sight on the canal, moving sedately in such striking contrast to the roar and rush of the train. Rome is but six miles away on the west, Utica nine miles on the east. Across the valley the hills rise gently in alternate farm and forest, with the spire of more than one village church pricking above the greenery.

"This battle of Oriskany," said our friend musingly, "would be considered a mere skirmish in our day, but it wrought ulterior results of the greatest importance. Down there in the Mohawk Valley at Herkimer, twenty-four miles distant, in 1725 a colony of German Palatines from the Rhenish Palatinate had been settled. As has been well said, because they were so well used to fire, and sword, battle, siege, and massacre at home, they could better stand the savage incursions to which that frontier fort was then exposed.

"Among these Palatines was a certain John Jost Herkimer, or properly Hercheimer, who had a son Nicholas, who in 1776 had risen to be a leader among his people, and for that reason had been appointed Brigadier-General of the militia of Tryon County. The British plan of battle directed Burgoyne to march down Lake Champlain, and Colonel St. Leger with an auxiliary force to enter the Mohawk Valley at its head and move down it, swelling his column with the

Tories and Indians who were numerous then, and
gathering from its rich fields supplies for the main
column, which he was to join at Albany.   On the 16th
of July Herkimer heard that St. Leger had appeared
at Oswego with a large force bent on this expedition,
and he at once issued his proclamation calling for
volunteers to repel the invader.   On the 4th of August
he set out with 800 men to meet the foe who had in-
vested Fort Stanwix, which stood yonder in the valley
near the present site of Rome.   St. Leger, apprised of
his coming, sent forward his Tories and Indians to
form an ambush in yonder ravine, and in the heavy
timber which then covered this hill.   Herkimer's van
guard came marching along the road yonder, little
suspecting danger, when suddenly they were saluted
with a volley and the deafening yells of the savages.
Fortunately the German farmers were untrammeled
by discipline.   They broke ranks at once, and fought
as their enemies fought, from tree to tree and from
rock to rock.   For five long hours the battle continued.
Herkimer's white horse was early killed under him,
and he was mortally wounded; he directed his saddle
to be placed on a fallen tree and calmly sat on it, smoking his pipe and commanding the battle.   Two hundred of the patriots lay dead, when suddenly the
savages lost heart and fled, giving the day to the brave
Herkimer and his followers.   St. Leger's march was
stayed.   Burgoyne, deprived of his ally, and of the

expected provisions, surrendered, and Continental affairs assumed an entirely new phase."

Mr. Lewis took us to a spot on the hillside near the ravine and pointed out the site of the tree on which Herkimer sat to direct the battle, and then into the ravine to see a corduroy road hastily laid by General Herkimer on the day of the battle for his troops to cross. A ditch had recently been dug across it, cutting through some of the logs which were seen to be still in good heart. Several of them since the erection of the monument had been carried to the sawmill and sawn into canes, which had been quickly disposed of as relics of the fight.[1]

[1] This article was written in 1883.

CHAPTER XIII

JOHNSON HALL[1]

A S I sit at my window in the village hotel of Johnstown, I see across green meadows a fine old
country seat set on a little elevation in a pretty park
of native trees. The villagers know it as Johnson
Hall, the former seat of Sir William Johnson, Baronet.
Perhaps no house in the land has seen stranger vicissitudes. Council after council of red men has been
held within its walls; throngs of painted savages have
surrounded it, sometimes bent on merry-making,
sometimes on war. Settlers have fled to it for refuge.
In its old library for twelve long years centered all the
wires that directed the Indian affairs of the northern
colonies. Then spies were continually going out from
it into all the Indian country, and swift runners bearing belts or messages from the Canada tribes, from
the Ottawas, Wyandots, Senecas, and Shawnees, and
from the outposts of Detroit and along the lakes, were
continually arriving. It has been the scene too of a
generous hospitality. An Indian princess once presided there as its mistress, and entertained at her

[1] First appeared in the *New York Evening Post* in 1883.

board with equal courtesy titled visitors from foreign
lands, grave colonial gentlemen in wigs and ruffles,
and the blanketed chieftains of her own nation.
Groups of merry children, showing the lineaments of
the Caucasian father and Indian mother, have played
about its doors. It has been the scene of bridals,
births, and deaths, of stirring incidents, romantic
episodes, and diplomatic triumphs without number,
and now in more peaceful days preserves the stateli-
ness and dignity befitting a mansion with a history.
The old house stands on a slight elevation, about a
mile from the village, in a park of some ten acres, with
meadows and green fields sloping from it in every
direction. The approach is by a private road set with
shade trees. The park is well kept and fragrant with
flowers and shrubbery. Four great, gaunt poplars
stand within it which are pointed out as having been
planted by the Baronet himself, a year after the house
was built. A row of gnarled old lilac trees set in the
form of an ellipse, and still blooming in their season,
were set out by the same hand.

The Hall itself is a square-roofed two-story and
attic structure, built of wood clapboarded in the form
of blocks of stone, and at its best estate had two wings
built of solid stone and pierced for musketry; but one
of these, however, is now standing. On entering the
house its solidity and wide proportions at once mark
it as a product of the colonial era. Its timbers are

THE JOHNSON HOUSE
Reproduced from an old-time French print

massive. The hall running through the building is forty feet long by fifteen wide, with a broad staircase leading to a similar hall above. The rooms are high and spacious and the sides are wainscoted with heavy panels and carved work. On the roof is an observatory from which one may look into four counties. This, however, did not form a part of the original structure. Bow-windows in parlor and dining-room have also been added by the present owner. In other respects it stands precisely as it was left by its titled builder. It was built in 1763, and was then considered one of the finest mansions in the colony outside of New York.

Sir William Johnson came of a good family in Ireland and arrived in America in 1738, at the age of twenty-three, to take charge of a large estate in the Mohawk Valley which his uncle, Captain Peter Warren, had purchased some years before. Either through his own address or the influence of his family the young Irishman "got on" famously in the new world. He cleared lands, invited settlers, opened a country store, built a flouring mill, and drove a profitable trade with the Indians, and in a few years became favorably known not only in his own section but at Albany and New York. In a few years we find him receiving offices from the Crown, but that which secured him the favor of his Government and brought him wealth and honors was the unbounded influence which he soon acquired over his savage neighbors, the Six Nations. Perhaps no other man ever studied the Indian character, habits, and sympathies so thoroughly, or possessed such tact and skill in making use of his knowledge. To secure their friendship, he visited them in their villages, dressed in their garb, sat in their councils, seated them as guests at his own table, took part in their ceremonies, and allied himself domestically with one of their most powerful clans. He early saw the importance to the colony and to England of winning and holding this strong confederacy to the English cause, and that the man who could do this was sure of advancement and favor. He lived during the stirring period of the French and Indian wars. Wily emissaries of the French were continually appearing among the Six Nations, bribing them and striving to arouse their prejudices against their neighbors, the English; but during this entire period the influence of this one man held the Indians to their fealty and saved the colony from destruction. It was natural that he should be rewarded for this. As early as 1746 the chief management of Indian affairs was entrusted to him and he was given the command of several Indian expeditions against the French. In 1755 he was made a Major-General and given command of one of the four armies raised that year for service against the French, and after meeting and defeating Baron Dieskau on Lake George the Crown created

him a Baronet, while Parliament voted him five thousand pounds to support the honor. In addition he
had received at various times immense tracts of land.
In 1762 he was the owner, either by purchase or grant,
of nearly all the fertile region now included in the
county of Fulton, and about this time settled one
hundred families on the site of the present village of
Johnstown, and partly for their protection and partly
to maintain a better espionage over the Indians built
the old mansion which I have described. The scene
then was far different from that presented now. A
heavy forest covered the country, broken only by the
clearing about the little settlement, and bear and
panther, Mohawk, Delaware, and Seneca prowled in it.

The Hall was scarcely completed when it became
the scene of a notable Indian council. In the summer
of 1762 Pontiac, King of the great Ottawa Confederacy,
had formed a design of driving the English from the
country and had invited all the great interior tribes,
among them the Six Nations, to join with him in the
enterprise. The Senecas alone were seduced from
their allegiance, many of their braves being engaged
with Pontiac in the attacks which were made that year
on the English outposts in the West. The chiefs of
the five nations, unsolicited by Johnson, went to re-
monstrate with the offending tribe, but they found its
young men averse to remaining at peace with the English. A few of their clans, however, had not gone on

the war path, and these desired the intercession of the
ambassadors that they might be spared in the chastise-
ment which they were sure the English would inflict
on their nation, and it was arranged that six of the
friendly Senecas should return with the embassy to
Johnson Hall and present their claims in person.
The conference was held on the 7th of September.
Three hundred and twenty delegates from the five
nations with the six friendly Senecas in all the bravery
of paint and feathers attended it. Johnson, attired
in the full uniform of Major-General, gave the head
chiefs an audience in the drawing-room of the old
mansion. The Onondaga chief opened the council
with a speech in which he graphically depicted the
whole course of the mission and the present hostile
attitude of the Senecas, introduced in fitting terms
the envoys of the peaceful clans, and dwelt eloquently
on the loyalty of the five nations to the English despite
the specious promises of Pontiac. Johnson's reply
showed the finesse of the accomplished diplomat. He
commended the loyalty of the five nations in their
efforts to bring the Senecas to reason, and reminded
them that the latter were not only enemies to the English
but traitors to the Confederacy, since they interrupted
its trade and disturbed its friendly relations with the
English. He might justly ask them to take up the
hatchet against the delinquents, but only desired them
to remain quiet and observe how the English punished

their enemies. Turning to the friendly Senecas, he commended their individual loyalty, but gave them to understand that, as their nation was in open rebellion, any clemency that might be shown them would be due to the intercession of their confederates. The council broke up with the fealty of the five great nations during Pontiac's war secured.

Close on the heels of this council came an embassy from the Ganniagwaris, a people of the same stock as the Mohawks, but now residing on the Saint Lawrence, praying for redress from the Jesuits, who had seized some of their richest lands by virtue of a patent from Louis XIV. The Baronet promised to lay their grievance before the King, and then began the task of enlisting them on the English side in a war against Pontiac. They replied figuratively, referring to their disarmament by the English in the last French War. "When you took the war axe from us you directed us to pursue our hunting, so that we must now be still, having no axe." In reply Sir William presented them with an axe of the best English steel and directed them to pass it around among their warriors with instructions to use it in cutting off all the bad links which had sullied the chain of friendship. The embassy returned, and in a few days their three hundred braves were on the war path against Pontiac.

But the most notable council ever held here was that of 1768, between the Six Nations and their ancient

enemies, the Cherokees. In December, 1767, three
Cherokee chiefs arrived at Albany by sloop from New
York, and, accompanied by Colonel Philip Schuyler,
proceeded on horseback to Johnson Hall, their object
being to arrange a treaty of peace between their nation
and the Confederacy. The Baronet entertained them
in state, and at once despatched the belt by runners
to call a grand council of the tribes. On the third of
March a large body of the confederates and their allies
had been gathered at the Hall. They came out of the
dense forest singly and by twos and threes, Delawares,
Shawnees, Senecas, and Mohawks, with laggard steps
and lowering brows, and gathered about the Hall,
until seven hundred and sixty warriors had surrounded
it. No man ever had a more formidable task appointed
him than had the Baronet in moving this large assembly
to his will. The entire Confederacy was in a ferment
this time over the outrages committed upon it by the
English. Its lands had been seized, its members
jeered and insulted, and many of them murdered by
settlers. No notice had been taken of their offer to
cede all their lands east of the Ohio for a small consideration, and the colonies were on the verge of another
terrible Indian war. The Baronet, however, held
several private interviews with the principal chiefs
before the grand council took place, at which he told
them among other things that he had received certain
intelligence that the King had decided to accept their

offer to sell the lands east of the Ohio, and so far won them to good humor that at the council the treaty with the Cherokees was concluded.

These were a few of the many councils and private meetings of chiefs of which the old Hall has been the scene. Disputes and questions of various kinds, such as were continually arising on the border, were also brought here for settlement. Petty differences between Indian and white man, land claims involving thousands of acres, were here decided, and criminal actions conducted.

Despite his public duties the Baronet found time for a genial and generous hospitality. Few gentlemen of the colony or foreign visitors of rank or note came into the Mohawk Valley without being entertained under his roof. Among the latter was Lord Adam Gordon, who afterward became Commander-in-Chief of the army in Scotland, and between whom and his host a firm friendship was established. Another titled visitor was Lady Susan O'Brian, eldest daughter of Stephen Fox, first Earl of Ilchester, and sister of Lady Harriet Ackland.

The mistress of the mansion during these years was an Indian princess, a sister of the celebrated Mohawk chief Thayendanega. She first attracted the Baronet's attention at a militia training, where, a beautiful, sprightly girl of sixteen, she won the plaudits of the multitude by leaping at the invitation of an officer to the crupper of his horse and riding with him in a mad gallop about the parade ground. About 1750 the Baronet and she were married according to the Indian custom, although it is not probable that the English ceremony was ever performed. The lady is described as being agreeable in person and as possessing sound understanding. Lady O'Brian speaks of her in her letters as a well-bred and agreeable lady, who in many rambles about the forests proved herself a pleasant companion. Sir William's chief object in the alliance, no doubt, was to secure greater influence with the Indian chiefs, but the lady seems to have made him a faithful wife, and the pair lived together in the greatest harmony until the husband's death.

This event occurred suddenly in the library of the old house on the 9th of July, 1774. During the day the Baronet had stood two hours in the burning July sun, delivering a speech to several hundred Indians who had assembled to ask his aid in seeking redress for encroachments on their lands. At the conclusion of the address he was seized with a violent attack of dysentery and conveyed to his library, where he died in the arms of a faithful attendant almost before his family could reach the scene. This was the last event worthy of note in the history of the old mansion. In the troubles which quickly followed, the Baronet's family espoused the royal cause and the Hall became an object of suspicion and dislike to the patriot leaders. It, however, happily escaped the torch during the war, and remains one of the few colonial houses with a history saved to the student of to-day.

CHAPTER XIV

THE thousands that daily whirl by New Rochelle on the trains of the Consolidated Railroad see little more than the earth and stone walls of a deep cut, and up on the bank to the right a stone church surrounded by an ancient churchyard. If one leaves the train for a day's ramble, he finds beyond the stone walls and the church a large town, with many fine old country-seats, and as many modern villas, wide business and residence streets, and as many narrow ones lined with humbler dwellings.

A road stretches north away from the town eight miles to the village of White Plains and its ancient battle-ground — a highway made smooth and hard by its covering of broken stone, winding between ranks of tall, ragged locusts, their tops dead and broken off, through a beautiful and highly cultivated region.

One passes here a country seat, there a new villa smart with a coat of parti-colored paint; just beyond a little cottage with stone walls and gables, low, antiquated

[1] Written in 1885.

porch, green wooden shutters, and huge chimney that must have been built for one of the Huguenot yeomen who settled New Rochelle over two centuries ago.

At one place, on a bluff in thick woods, is an old, deserted house that has been without human habitant to care for it for generations, and where, in Revolutionary days, when the cowboys and skinners harried all this region, an old man and his daughter were tortured and left for dead in the effort to make them reveal the depository of their secret hoards.

By all the rules of apparitions this house should be haunted, but on inquiry the pilgrim could find no record of so much as a ghostly light or footfall ever being seen or heard there.

A mile of this road, and then the tourist pauses on the side of a hill whose summit is crowned with handsome dwellings and fine farms, before a marble shaft set in a space some twelve feet square, with an iron fence in front and a solid wall of stone enclosing it from the meadow behind, and from a lane that turns in on the north side, and after dipping down to cross a brook, ascends the hill to a modest, low-walled farmhouse that with its outbuildings occupies the summit.

On the western face of the monument, next the road, is a medallion likeness of Thomas Paine, with the inscription:

"Thomas Paine,
Author of 'Common Sense.'
Born in England, January 29, 1737,
Died in New York city, June 8, 1809.
'The palaces of kings are built upon the ruins of the
bowers of Paradise.' — *Common Sense*."

Above the medallion is Paine's motto:

"The world is my country,
To do good my religion."

The south side bears quotations from the Crisis
No. I. and from Crisis No. XV. The inscriptions on
the east and north sides are taken from the "Age of
Reason." Fertile meadows sweep away to the eastward, cut in twain by the farm-road mentioned. They
form part of the estate given to Paine in 1783 by the
State of New York for his services in the Revolution.

The history of both monument and farm is interesting. Paine, as he lay on his dying bed, evinced considerable anxiety as to the disposal of his body after
death, fearing, perhaps, that it would not meet with
proper respect. His father was a Quaker, and he
desired to be laid to rest in the burying-ground of that
people. He sent to Mr. Willet Hicks, a respectable
Quaker living near, and said that, as he was going to
leave one place, it was necessary to provide another,
and wished to be interred in the Quaker burying-
ground, adding that he might be interred in the Epis-

The Thomas Paine Memorial

copal churchyard, but they were so arrogant, or in the Presbyterian, but they were so hypocritical. The Quakers, however, refused the desired permission.

In his last will and testament, dated January 18, 1809, Paine expressed a wish to be buried in the Quaker burying-ground if they permitted it, but if they would not allow it he wished to be buried on his farm, "the place where I am to be buried to be a square of twelve feet, to be enclosed with rows of trees and a stone or post and rail fence, with a headstone with my name and age engraved upon it, 'Author of Common Sense.'" He was so buried in a plot in the field a few yards south of the present monument. In 1819, however, William Cobbett, the great English Liberal, while in this country dug up his bones and carried them to England, but what disposition was made of them is not known. In 1838–9 funds for the present monument were raised by public subscription, and the marble was cut at Tuckahoe. When those having the matter in charge came to erect it, they were forbidden by the owner to cross his land to the grave, the farm now having passed into strange lands, and after some delay the present site was purchased and the stone was erected there.

After a time the monument fell into neglect. Those who had known Paine, or who remembered the facts attending its erection, had died or removed. A few years ago the stone was used as a bill-board, and was literally covered with handbills and posters. At length a movement was set on foot in New York and New Rochelle, funds were collected sufficient to restore it, and in 1881 it was rededicated with appropriate ceremonies and the present inscriptions.

The farm in the days preceding the Revolution was known as the "Devoe Farm," and was owned by Frederick Devoe. "Yeoman," he is styled in the early records. Frederick Devoe was a Tory, and according to tradition piloted the British troops over the country roads to White Plains in 1776, where they intrenched. For this offense he was indicted for treason November 10, 1780, and judgment was declared against him July 5, 1783, whereupon his farm was confiscated under the Confiscation Act, and given by the State of New York to Thomas Paine. Cheatham, in his 'Life of Paine,' says: "The farm contained more than 300 acres of land, and an elegant stone house 120 x 28 feet." In point of fact the farm lacked some twenty acres of 300, and the house was far from "elegant," being a small stone farmhouse of a story and a half, such as sheltered the yeomen of that day. The original structure, considerably modified and improved, may be studied in the farmhouse which we have mentioned as standing on the summit of the hill to the eastward of the monument.

Calling on Mr. Wesley Lee, the then proprietor, we were shown the parlor which Paine occupied, and

the library opening out of it in which he wrote. These
have been little changed from the time of the author's
occupancy. "When I bought it," said Mr. Lee, "the
only relics of Paine remaining were the old Franklin
stove and andirons he used; the stove still set in the
brickwork in the library. These I let Mr. Walter Bell,
the stove-dealer in New Rochelle, have in exchange
for a modern stove and appurtenances. I presume
he still has them."

Returning to New Rochelle, we called on Mr. Bell,
and were shown the stove, which, if it had never belonged to Paine, would still possess interest as being
the first form that took shape in the inventor's mind.
It is composed of heavy upright and horizontal plates
of iron held in place by grooves, there not being a bolt
or rod in the whole fabric — a sort of iron box, in which,
on andirons, the fire was built. Mr. Bell has two
affidavits to prove that the stove was really Paine's.
One is from Mr. Lee, stating that at the time he purchased the property there was a Franklin stove set in
the brickwork of the room on the northeast corner of
the house, and a pair of andirons, and that he made
inquiry of the former owners, and also of old residents,
and from information thus obtained he believed them
to be the same as those formerly used by Thomas
Paine. The other is from Augustus Van Cortlandt,
M.D., a former resident of New Rochelle, who says
that "in the year 1841 he was taken by his father to

the house formerly occupied by Thomas Paine, author of the 'Age of Reason,' 'Common Sense,' and the 'Rights of Man'; that while there he was shown the old Franklin stove and andirons, which his father stated were seen by him in the year 1808, when he presented a letter to Thomas Paine personally in the same room where said Franklin stove and andirons were, and that from the design and certain marks thereon he knows them to be the articles shown him as aforesaid, and that the same are now in possession of Messrs. Bell and Harmer."

"My object in getting these affidavits," continued Mr. Bell, "was to prove the authenticity of the relics, and it was suggested to me by the fact that on my way home with the stove I met a man, a citizen of New Rochelle, who laughed at the very idea that I had Paine's stove in the wagon. Dr. Van Cortlandt was a member of the old Van Cortlandt family, a learned and respectable gentleman, who told me a great many things about Paine. He said that when his father called on the latter he was clad in a dressing-gown that had evidently been made of a blanket, and with a beard of three days' growth on his face. A deal table stood in the room, without a cover, on which was a part of a loaf of bread, a pitcher of milk, and a bowl of molasses, from which his breakfast had evidently been furnished. He said that there was valuable

furniture and bric-à-brac in the room, including a
fine French clock, medals given to Paine by various
societies, with bronzes and medallions.   He said Paine
once made a model of an iron bridge to cross the
Harlem River at a single span, which was thought a
wonderful thing in those days.   The only other relic
of Paine now in New Rochelle, so far as I know, is an
old armchair in which he sat during his frequent calls
on his neighbors, the Badeaus, who lived nearly opposite the monument.   Mrs. Badeau, who lived to be
quite aged, always spoke of Paine with the greatest
esteem and respect, though she did not share in his
religious views.   He had a love for little children, she
said, that almost amounted to a passion, and was in
turn a great favorite with them.   She described him
as pleasant and social in familiar intercourse, with a
fund of anecdote and information, on which he was
always willing to draw for the entertainment of his
friends.   The last years of this good old lady were
spent in protecting the grave and tombstone of her
friend from the attacks of curiosity and relic-hunters.
Often has she raised her window and frightened off
men who were breaking chips from edges of the stone,
to be preserved as relics.   She saw Cobbett's men when
they rifled the grave in 1819, and warned them away,
but they refused to go, saying they were acting under
Cobbett's orders.

"I know of but one person now living in the town

who remembers Paine. That person is Mrs. Davenport, a very aged lady living on Davenport's Neck. She says that Paine often patted her on the head when she was a little girl."

CHAPTER XV

THE AMERICAN BARBISON

BARBISON, the well-known resort of so many French artists and art-students, where Millet and a whole colony of painters have found inspiration and subjects worthy of their pencils, lies in the heart of the ancient forest of Fontainebleau, at an easy distance from the great capital. Easthampton,[1] which we have ventured to call the American Barbison, is a village of Puritan origin, situated at the southeastern extremity of Long Island, in a little oasis of meadows and wheat-fields, that owes some portion of its attractiveness to its surroundings of sand and scrub. Its one wide main street is so prodigal of land that it could only have been laid out by men with a continent at their disposal. Great elms and willows overarch it, and beyond their vistas the eye rests on the broad bosom of the Atlantic, flecked by summer sails. Northward one looks on orchards and green fields. The dwellings that line it for a mile please by their endless variety. There is the quaint old Puritan cottage, with

[1] Written in 1883. Easthampton is now a fashionable and exclusive resort and the conditions here pictured no longer exist.

its gables facing the street, and flanked by the wood-
shed and mossy well-sweep and bucket. There are
square, roomy, old-fashioned farmhouses, some newly
painted, some dingy and moss-covered, with low stoops
opening directly upon the street. There is a quaint
old village academy, the first opened in the State.
There are little shops that nobody knows the use of,
an inn, a few summer villas, a fine old country-seat
standing remote and grand behind a copse of maples
and cedars, and at either end of the village street a
windmill, — gaunt, weather-beaten structures, that at
the merest suspicion of a breeze throw their long arms
as wildly and creak and clatter as noisily as those that
Don Quixote attacked. The old church, built in 1717,
in whose turret hung a bell presented by Queen Anne,
— one of the historical churches of the land, — was
pulled down in 1872, its demolition marking an epoch
in the town's existence. The churchyard, once under
the wing of the church, is now set lonesomely in the
midst of the main street, its white tombstones looked
down upon by all the neighboring dwellings and con-
stantly reminding the villagers of the virtues of their
ancestors. Still, it is an interesting spot, with its fence
of palings, its quaint old-fashioned stiles, and mossy
stones, whose legends tell of wrecks upon the coast,
and of brave young spirits drowned at sea, killed by
falling from the masthead, crushed in the whale's
jaws, or fever-stricken and buried in some tropical

MAIN STREET, EASTHAMPTON
Looking southward. From a photograph by E. B. Muchmore

island. In a place so remote, it is natural that the quaintness and pastoral simplicity of country life a hundred years ago should still prevail. At sunset and sunrise herds of sleek, matronly cows, with barefoot boys in attendance, wind through the street; scythes and sickles hang in the willows by the wayside; and every morning the mail-coach rattles into the village with a musical flourish of the driver's horn, stops at the post-office for the mail-bag, calls all along the street for bags, baskets, and parcels, and at last rumbles away toward the railway station, seven miles distant. Most truly rural are the orchard farmyards, which abut upon the street without concealment, in front perhaps set thickly with apple- and pear-trees, and behind these showing open spaces covered with a deep greensward, with cart, plow, stack, wood-pile, sheep, and poultry disposed in picturesque confusion.

Our village, in its two hundred years of existence, has gathered about it an atmosphere of legend and romance, and one may still see with the mind's eye some of the quaint figures and striking scenes of its early history. One can easily call up Parson James, the first minister ("Gent." he is styled in the old records), walking to church in wig and gown, — or Mistress Abigail Hedges riding down on her wedding-day to Sagg, four miles distant, and on the way counting thirteen whales sporting in the surf. An excited throng in the streets, and Parson James led away

under arrest to New York for denouncing in the
pulpit the exorbitant tax levied on "whale's oyle and
fins" by the governor of the colony; a detachment of
British troops in possession of the town, and Sir William
Erskine, Governor Tryon, Lord Percy, Lord Cathcart,
Major André, in brilliant uniforms, pacing under the
village elms; the old Hunting tavern, in which the
young officers made merry with the wits and roysterers
of the village, even old "Sharper" the slave being
admitted to add his shrewd pleasantries and unequaled
powers of mimicry to the general hilarity; a drawing-
room in the old Gardiner mansion, with Sir Henry
Clinton present, and André at his request entertaining
the company with a recital of his sparkling ballad of
"Chevy Chase"; Parson Beecher on a Friday hieing
away to the beaches for a day's shooting, forgetting
the preparatory lecture, and, when reminded by the
bell, hurrying to the church, setting down his gun in
the porch, and preaching in his hunting-suit with an
unction that never attended his written sermons; the
old parsonage, and the parson in his study drawing
strains from his beloved violin; Madam Beecher's
pretty girl-pupils in the schoolroom above tapping
their little feet in unison with the music, and at last
breaking into the forbidden dancing step, causing the
violin to cease with a doleful screech; a low-ceiled
kitchen, with deep fireplace and smoky walls, in which
John Howard Payne composed the song that has

excelled all others in popularity, and wrote love-letters
to one of the village maidens, — letters still preserved
in rose and lavender; President Tyler riding in a grand
sort of way up the street to woo and win a maiden in
one of the village mansions: — these are but a few
of the old-time scenes that pass in review before the
eyes of the dreamer under the village elms. This
charm of old associations combined with pastoral simplicity is evanescent, and will soon be gone. Already
the railroad, rude iconoclast, is approaching, to destroy
the relics of the past and change the whole aspect
of the place. The limner, therefore, who succeeds in
depicting such features as are best worth preserving
will not have performed an unappreciated task.

The summer phase of the village is almost entirely
artistic. What painter first discovered it is a subject
for speculation; but when discovered its possibilities
in the way of art rapidly became known, and it has
been for several years the summer home of many
favorites of the public. Last season the little colony
of artists had become fairly domiciled by the 1st of
July: T—— in a cottage on the main street, whose
interior and antique furniture were to yield inspiration
for several studies of the olden time; "Dante" and his
young wife in the old village academy, which had long
ceased to be an academic haunt; "the Count" and
"the Doctor" in sweet proximity to a confectioner's
shop; "Mozart" at the inn; and the others scattered

about in the boarding-houses of the village. Two
sketching-classes added a progressive feature, — one
comprising several ladies of the Art Students' League
of New York, who were domiciled at first in a cottage
by the sea, and, later, in the village inn; while the
other, also composed of ladies, met three times weekly
in the former schoolroom of the academy. Dante
alone achieved a studio. It was on the upper floor
of the academy, and presented a medley of "studies,"
nets, rusty anchors, spoils of the sea, flowers, birds'
nests, and trophies won from the village houses, —
poke bonnets, stocks, perukes, faded gowns, armchairs, spinning-wheels, and other ancient furniture.
This became a favorite gathering-place with members
of the craft, and, during the summer, witnessed the
reunions of many long-sundered friends. Besides the
artists, a score or so of quiet families made the place
their summer quarters; but its characteristic features
remained the same, — in every quiet nook and coigne
of vantage an artist with his easel, fair maidens trudg-
ing afield with the attendant small boy bearing easel,
color-box, and other *impedimenta*, sketching-classes
setting out in great farm-wagons carpeted with straw,
white-aproned nurse-maids, rosy babies, and pleasure-
vehicles in the streets.

The routine for the summer was tolerably uniform.
Out-door work was usually done in the soft light and
shade of early morning or evening. In-door work

occupied a part of the intervening hours if the artist
was industrious.   At eleven there was a gathering on
the bathing-beach, and an hour's wild sporting with
the surges of the Atlantic.   There was tennis for those
who cared for it, straw-parties and sailing-parties,
moonlight rides to the beach, excursions to Sagg,
Hardscrabble, Pantago, and Amagansett.   The students
of the sketching-classes were the most industrious,
wandering about the village, selecting their subjects, sketching, painting, and returning to the inn at
night with their spoils.   Sometimes the great carryall
carried them out to Tyler's for a day's sketching.
Arrived there, one drew the quaint old dilapidated
barn, another the farmyard, a third the mossy well-
sweep, a fourth the crooked-necked duck leading her
brood to water, a fifth the grain-fields, and so on, till
all were supplied with subjects.   At intervals the
grave professor came to the inn and passed on the
students' work with his pungent criticisms.   There
was a large wheat-field on the southern rim of the town,
near the sea, that attracted many visitors and gave
rise to more day-dreams than any palace of the genii.
Its black mold closed on the white sand of the beach,
and there was little interval between the bearded
wheat and the coarse bunchgrass of the dunes.   It
seemed a novel sight, this strong young daughter of
the West drawing life and nourishment from the
grizzled ocean.   Such points of similarity as should

exist between sire and daughter were often noted by
imaginative visitors. When the wind blew, there were
waves in the wheat as well as in the sea; argosies of
cloud-shadows sailed over it, and it never lost a low,
soft murmur, that seemed a faint refrain of the vast
monotone of the sea. What weird imaginations and
startling effects, to be elaborated in the studio on the
return to the city, were suggested by it, cannot be told.
The beach, with its broad reaches of sand and foaming
surges, its wrecks, sand-storms, mirages, soft colors,
and long line of sand dunes cut into every variety of
fantastic shape by the winds, was equally prolific of
wild fancies.

If this routine became at all prosaic or commonplace,
it was soon broken by some ludicrous incident while
at the easel, — the unearthing of a new character, or
subjugation of a refractory model: all of which was
sure to be related with gusto at the post-prandial
re-unions in the "bird's-nest."

Wonderfully numerous and varied are the "characters" of the village; and this adds largely to its artistic
value. Old farmers with their homely saws, grizzled
whalemen, fishermen, and wreckers and life-saving
men, may all be met here. There are "originals,"
indigenous to the soil. No one who has ever sum-
mered in Barbison will forget the Remuslike face of
Uncle Pete, the childlike and bland countenance of
"Old Zeb," the sly twinkle in the eye of Sam Green,

the village joker, or the grim smile that rests on the
face of "Old Hominy" in the midst of his cutest trick.

To give a perfect idea of the artistic features of our
village, one must speak somewhat in detail of the
relations of the artists with these characters. Uncle
Pete, the village octogenarian, is the favorite and
most troublesome model. The old man lives alone,
in a little bunk of a cottage, on the outskirts of Free-
town, — a settlement of colored people about a mile
north of the village. Having made five whaling
voyages in his youth, Uncle Pete has acquired a store
of reminiscences, which he has a Remuslike fondness
for retailing to his numerous callers. His tall, almost
majestic figure, and black, shrewd, quizzical face
looking out from a mass of snow-white wool, tickle the
artistic fancy, and his lineaments have been preserved
on more canvases than those of the most popular
model in the Latin quarter. This popularity has made
him extremely coy and uncertain; and the artist who
would engage him, in addition to the offer of golden
shekels, must often have recourse to personal blandishments. The old man generally prefers to pose in the
doorway of his little cottage: for ten minutes he sits
quietly, and his outlines begin to appear under the
pencil; then he grows restless, and begins to fidget,
whereupon his employer, scenting trouble, blandly
asks for a story. Uncle Pete readily complies, entertaining his auditor with a graphic account of his

descent into the whale's jaws once upon a time in Delagoa Bay, his countenance meanwhile assuming an animated and expressive cast. The tale concluded the sitter again becomes restless, and is asked for another story, which he readily narrates. A third or fourth perhaps will be required before the sitting is finished. Old Zeb, another model, is what the villagers call a "natural," although he has wit enough to gain a living without much labor. He is a great favorite with the ladies, and, being quite susceptible, has made several propositions of a matrimonial nature to engaging damsels visiting the village, which are understood to be under consideration. At sunset on pleasant evenings, when his fair friends are sure to be found on the front porches, Zeb is seen wending his way through the street with a rose in his button-hole, roses in his hand, and a basket on his arm. The ladies greet him graciously, and in their sweetest tones beg for a song. Zeb complies, seated on the ground, nursing his knees with his hands, and chanting in a weird monotone some hymn or ballad of the olden time. The song ended, his fair patrons bestow small coins, and, murmuring his thanks in a fine feminine voice, he moves on to another coterie. It generally happens, however, that, while the song is in progress, some deft knight of the brush has transferred his lineaments to the sketch-book for future use. Often a party goes down to Zeb's cottage at the "Harbor" to sketch him

at his weekly "shave." The old fellow is very proud
of his smoothly-shaven face, and takes great pride in
its preservation. His Saturaday "shave" is a marvel
of the tonsorial art. While it is in progress he is seated
in the doorway of his cottage, with a little hand looking-glass before him, and a great Mambrino's helmet
of a wash-hand-basin filled with hot water by his side.
His razor, "borrerd" for the occasion, has been through
several whaling-voyages. Having honed it on the door-
sill, he assaults his stubby beard vigorously, grubbing
and grubbing with an expression on his face that con-
vulses the spectators. He explains "that it don't
take hold well, somehow," and stops to sharpen his
instrument on the grindstone. The entire operation
is enlivened by a running fire of comments and queries
from the spectators, to which Zeb returns the most
amusing and innocent replies. Pat's "childers" are
desirable but most refractory models. There are
several of them running wild about the street, little
Patseys and Bridgets, red-haired, freckled, snub-
nosed, barefooted, so humorously and grimly defiant that
they tickle the artistic fancy and are much coveted as
models. Mrs. Pat, however, when approached on the
subject, discovers a feminine quality which has time
and again brought the artist into difficulties. "Be-
gorra," she declares, "ef yez artises are after the childer,
it's not in thim dirty clothes they'll be tooken. If the'r
picters are tooken at all, it must be in the'r Sundays

best." This is entirely inadmissible, and the painter is obliged to waylay his models as they run, and induce them to sit by a liberal supply of taffy and pop-corn.

An old weather-beaten dwelling at the upper end of the village street has been so often sketched and painted that it is a witticism of the guild when a new artist comes to town that Dominy's is going onto the canvas. Its clapboards are warped by over a century's exposure, a few bricks are missing from the chimney, some of the window-panes are gone, but all such disfigurements are hidden by a luxuriant growth of climbing plants. Two workshops, one flanking each side of the cottage, present curious interiors, — low ceilings, dusty, cobwebbed windows, tools of various callings disposed on the walls or in cribs in the ceiling, and a medley of articles scattered about,— old-fashioned clocks in long cases, a photographer's camera, a Damascus blade, with gold-inlaid hilt, fashioned into a chisel, nets, spears, lances, harpoons, and similar paraphernalia. In this dwelling lives one of the marked characters of the village, a universal genius, a master of all trades. He is the village miller, a farmer, a carpenter, a shipwright, a clock-maker, a tooth-puller, a photographer, a whaleman, a fisherman, and an office-holder. With the artists he is a prime favorite, and generally accompanies them as courier and guide in their sketching-excursions, whether by land or water. His shop is a favorite lounging-place of the

guild. The old man receives his visitors with a queer
mixture of fatherly kindness, assumed carelessness,
and "chaff." "You fellers," he observes, "git a thousand dollars in York for a picter of my back door, and
I git nothin'." To the modest request for leave to
paint his shop he replies that "there's been paint
enough wasted on it a'ready to ha' painted it inside
and out," but gives a grudging permission. Sometimes he "fixes it up" for the artist. Sometimes he
poses; again it is his dog Jack, the ugliest of canines,
or his boy Zi, that is in request. A thousand tales of
our hero's adventures and eccentricities are current in
the studios, in not a few of which the narrators were
the actors, and in some the victims. To turn the
laugh on his protégés is the height of the old man's
ambition: not infrequently the artist, sketching his
shop, on returning from dinner finds every article in
it removed to a different position, and some even hung
outside. His fishing-trip to Napeague last summer
with a party of artists is embalmed among the traditions
of the colony. Question the old man on the subject,
and his only reply is a chuckle. The victims when
approached manifest extreme reticence: it is known,
however, that they caught no fish, that they rowed
instead of sailing, owing to a dead calm, and that returning they reached the inn at one in the morning and forced a surreptitious entry through one
of its windows, the grand finale discovering the

hungry tramps in a fierce attack on the pies of the pantry.

A town meeting is sure to bring a rich harvest of "studies" into the village, especially if the questions to be discussed are of a broad public interest, such, for instance, as the pasturage of cattle in the village streets, or the extension of farmlands into the wide highway; these questions concern the commonalty, and there is a general hegira of the male portion of the outlying districts to the village. They come on foot, on horseback and muleback, in buckboards and in great farm-wagons with a capacity of ten or more. Some are barefoot, some attired only in check shirt and corduroys, with heavy sombreros for head-gear. At these gatherings, as in all popular assemblies, the two great orders — patrician and plebeian — are represented; and while the leaders gather in the old town-hall to discuss the matter, the rank and file are deposed about on the church steps, under the elms, in the stores, smoking, spitting, lounging in a thousand picturesque attitudes. From this repose they are routed by their respective leaders and hurried into the hall whenever a vote is to be taken.

The annual spring meet on Montauk was the occasion of another influx of strangers into the town. This "meet" was held usually on the 20th of June, to enable the owners to select from the herds the cattle intended for fattening, which were then turned into

the fattening-fields.   Barbison was the rendezvous for
the "proprietors" of all the districts to the westward,
and, as they came riding in in detachments, but for
the diverse regimentals one might have fancied that
André's regulars had reappeared to storm the town.

No features of Barbison the past season were more
pleasant than the impromptu receptions — artistic
séances in the best sense of the word — held in Dante's
studio.   Artists, scholars, and journalists met here on
common ground.   The discussions, however, were
brilliant rather than profound, and the reminiscences
generally of a light and humorous character.   Many
of them detailed the ludicrous incidents and adventures
met with on sketching-excursions.   H—— had a truly
bucolic experience.   He was in a wide field, putting
in the sheep, daisies, and a particularly fine clump of
maples, when, as he had nearly finished his work, he
was suddenly prostrated by the old ram of the flock,
who had evidently tired of the artist's presence in his
demesnes.   H—— picked himself up, and, seeing the
ram still warlike, made a quick retreat to the fence,
which he succeeded in reaching only to witness Aries
march back to the easel and trample painting, brushes,
and etceteras into the dust.   C——, while walking
along a country lane with his color-box in hand, had
met a native who took him for a spectacle-vender and
inquired the price of his wares.   "I am out of spectacles," replied the artist, and went his way.   Next

day, returning to finish his sketch, he met the same
man, and was again asked the price of "glasses."
"The fact is, friend," said he, "I don't sell spectacles."
— "What dew yeou sell, then?" queried the rustic.
By way of reply, the artist opened his box and showed
the neatly-ranged vials of color. The querist gave
but a look, and exclaimed, in inimitable tones of dis-
gust, "Homepathy doctor, by thunder!" D——
called at a farmhouse one morning and asked permission to make a picture in the yard. "Yes, sir,"
replied the farmer; "go in. The's fifteen in there
a'ready; but I tell 'em all I keer for is a drift-way."
G—— claimed the honor of having sketched a queen.
She was scrubbing the floor of the village grocery at
the time, and as the sketch was completed a negro
lounged in with the news that King Pharaoh of the
Montauk tribe was dead. "That makes me queen!"
exclaimed the woman, who proved to be the old king's
widow; and, straightening up, she discarded mop and
brush and at once set out for her new kingdom amid
the wastes of Montauk.

Such is Barbison in summer. As the season advances, however, its aspect rapidly changes. Visitors
depart with the first chill winds of autumn. The
forests of scrub take on their autumnal tints, the grass
withers, loads of golden corn and rich-yellow pumpkins
rattle up to the farmhouse doors. The life-saving
men leave their snug homes in the village and take

their places in the stations, which are opened, warmed, and furnished in readiness for the possible shipwrecked mariner. Every night the patrols keep their lonely vigils along shore. By and by it is seen that a storm is imminent: the sun sets behind a mass of gray, watery vapor, the ocean chafes, a strong wind, damp and rheumy, comes murmuring up from the southeast. At midnight, perhaps, the tempest breaks, howling down the chimneys, rattling the panes, swaying the little willows till they snap like a farmer's whip, and sending great waves up the beach to the base of the sand-dunes. Not infrequently on such nights the villagers are startled by the booming of a gun, telling that a wreck is on the bar.

In old times this was a signal for the most active preparations. The church bell was rung and a great horn blown to rally the surfmen to the beach. The housewives built fires, made coffee, and prepared stores of lint, comfortables, and flannels. If the surf permitted, the men rowed out to the ship and rescued the shipwrecked seamen, who were brought half dead to the village homes and tenderly cared for; but too often this was impossible, and windrows of dead bodies were gathered on the beach in the morning and laid stark and stiff in the coroner's office to be prepared for burial. As might be expected, some grewsome tales of the sea are to be heard in the village. A storm or wreck brings out a flood of such reminiscences. There are stories of similar incidents, of pirates and hidden treasures, of false lights set on the headlands; but quite as often the tales turn on wreckage and the flotsam and jetsam of the sea,— how a stately East-Indiaman would lay her ribs on the beach and spill her precious cargo of silks, cashmeres, pearls, teas, spices, and sandal-wood in the surf, a part of it, at least, to be gathered up by the daring wreckers. When a full-freighted whaleman came ashore, great cakes of pure white spermaceti were thrown far up the strand, and the whole country-side hurried to the scene with carts, wagons, sledges, and hand-barrows, to remove the precious product before it should melt. Sometimes it was coals from a lumbering collier that the men gathered up, sometimes lumber from a Maine bark, and again the ivory and gold-dust of Africa.

CHAPTER XVI

ONE who has had occasion to visit many rural churchyards must surely have been impressed by the great number of eminent Americans entombed in them. In the old world one seeks the tombs of the great beneath the most magnificent fanes, but our great men seem to have preferred rural solitudes for their last long sleep. There is an old unpretentious burial-ground in Litchfield, Connecticut, filled with quaint tombstsones of slate or sandstone so mossy and old that one with difficulty deciphers the names inscribed upon them; yet to write the biographies of the sleepers beneath them would be to write the history of the American nation itself. There is another at Lebanon, Connecticut, one at Quincy, Massachusetts, a fourth at Northampton, Massachusetts.

This old churchyard at Easthampton may be cited in support of the argument. It lies at the foot of the broad village main street, an arm of which encompasses either side. Its older stones date back to 1696 or earlier, and were imported from England, as the flying cherub, or death's head and scroll sculptured at the head attest.

Without doubt the oldest grave here is that of Lyon Gardiner, first lord of the manor of Gardiner's Island. His tomb, however, is new, having been erected a few years ago by his descendants. It is of pleasing and impressive design, a knight in complete armor laid upon a sarcophagus that rests in a little gothic temple of white marble. The inscription, covering all four sides of the tomb, will serve to show the flavor of antiquity possessed by our churchyard:

"In memory of Lion Gardiner, an officer of the English army, and an engineer and master of Works of Fortification in ye Leaguers of ye Prince of Orange in ye Low Countries in 1635. He came to New England in ye service of ye Company of Lords and Gentlemen. He builded and commanded ye Saybrook Forte. After accomplishing his term of service he removed in 1663, to his island of which he was sole owner and ruler. Born in 1599 he died in this town in 1663 venerated and honored."

A little south of the Gardiner tomb, and near the center of the churchyard, is a stone facing a different way from its neighbors and bearing this inscription:

"Mr. Thomas James dyed ye 6th day of June in ye yeare 1696. He was Minister of the Gospel and Pastore of the Church of Christ."

Parson James was the first pastor of the church at

Easthampton and served in that capacity over fifty
years. Tradition represents him as having been small
in stature, sprightly and undaunted in step and bearing, and very conscientious in the discharge of his
pastoral duties. That he might the better convert
the Indians who formed part of his parish, it is said
that he learned their language.

The fiber of the man is shown by his dying injunc-
tion, which was that he should be buried in a different
direction from his congregation, that on the resurrec-
tion morn he might arise facing his accusers (should
any impeach him as a pastor), as well as those who
had laughed to scorn his warnings and entreaties.
His last wish was complied with, as is seen by the
position of the grave.

His neighbor is the Rev. Samuel Buell, D.D., also
pastor of the Easthampton church for over half a century. The inscription on the heavy, brown-stone slab
above his grave is so similar in style to that written
by President Dwight for the tomb of General Israel
Putnam that I hazard the conjecture that they were
written by the same hand. Perhaps some of your
readers can speak definitely on the subject. It is as
follows: "Reader, behold this tomb with reverence and
regret. Here lie the remains of that eminent servant
of Christ, the Rev. Samuel Buell, D.D., fifty-three
years pastor of the church in this place. He was a
faithful and successful minister of the gospel, a kind

relative, a true friend, a good patriot, an honest man and an exemplary Christian, was born Sept. 1, 1716, died in peace July 19, 1798, aged eighty-two years.

"They that turn many to righteousness shall shine as the brightness of the firmament and the stars forever and ever.

"Remember them who have spoken unto you the word of God, whose faith follow, considering the end of their conversation."

Dr. Buell's term covered the perilous times of the revolution, and not a little of the immunity his parishioners enjoyed during the British occupancy of the island they owed to the doctor's influence over the English commander, Sir William Erskine, with whom he was a great favorite. Tradition says that on one occasion Sir William ordered a number of the farmers of Easthampton to go to Southampton to perform a certain work on the Sabbath.

In the interim he met the divine and told him that he had ordered out his parishioners on Sunday.

"I am aware of it," said the doctor, "but am myself commander-in-chief on that day, and have countermanded the order." It is said that Erskine, with a good-humored laugh, yielded the point.

Another anecdote is thus related: The young officers of Erskine's staff were fond of the chase, and Dr. Buell, who was something of a Nimrod, not infrequently joined them. On one occasion he was late, and the party had mounted when he arrived, but Sir William asked them to dismount and receive his guest. Lord Percy, Erskine's aide, later Duke of Northumberland, was impatiently pacing the floor when he was introduced to the doctor, who asked him civilly what part of his majesty's forces he had the honor to command.

"A legion of devils fresh from hell," replied Percy, who was nettled at the delay. "Then," said the doctor with his most stately bow, "I suppose I have the honor of addressing Beelzebub, prince of devils."

Percy laid his hand on his sword but was checked by Erskine, and during the ride that followed the divine paid such marked attention to the young officer and was so witty and agreeable that he won his regard and admiration.

The Mulford family gravestone reminds us that Easthampton was a pure republic for some years after its settlement, perhaps the purest ever known. We may be pardoned for dwelling on the fact since, unless we are greatly mistaken, it has wholly escaped the notice of political students.

Government was by town meeting — the general court — and by an inferior court called the "court of the three men." The town meeting was the supreme body: it constituted courts, tried important causes, heard appeals, chose the minister and schoolmaster, fixed their salaries, made police regulations, admitted

or excluded settlers, licensed taverns, opened highways, chose military officers and the whale watch, and
did what our lawmakers ought at once to do, fined all
freemen who refused or neglected to vote, to attend
town meeting, or to hold office when elected.

The court of the three men heard minor cases and
executed the laws, and in general carried on the affairs
of the town when the general court was not in session.
The executive officer was the constable who presided
at the town meetings and executed the commands of
both courts. The inferior court met at 8 A.M., on the
second day of the first week of every month for the
trial of cases.

Easthampton maintained this independent condition
for seven years, or until 1657, when she united with
the Connecticut colony.

One of the first justices of the inferior court was John
Mulford, who lies buried in the old churchyard. His
eldest son, Samuel Mulford, also rests here, a man
well worthy to rank with those whose iron wills and
stern courage gained their country's liberties. He was
the leader of the people's party in the Ninth Assembly
of New York during Governor Burnet's contest with
that body from 1715 to 1722.

For one of his speeches Burnet had him indicted
and prosecuted for sedition. Mulford, however, was
nowise daunted by this experience. Burnet had laid
a tax of one tenth on all the oil taken by the whaling

crews of Easthampton and Southampton — Mulford's
constituents — which he claimed as a perquisite.
Mulford determined to go to England and memo-
rialize Parliament for the removal of this tax.   He
sailed to Newport secretly, walked to Boston and
took ship for England, and read his memorial before
the House of Commons, which ordered the tax dis-
continued.

Returning in triumph, he was greeted with songs
and rejoicings by his constituents, and was promptly
returned by them to the Assembly.   Expelled by that
body, which was wholly subservient to the Governor,
he was reëlected and in the autumn of 1717 took his
seat in the House, being then seventy-three years of
age.

In 1720 he refused to act with the House of that
year, which he claimed had been illegally elected and
organized, and was again expelled.   This ended his
public service.   He died at Easthampton, August 21,
1725, aged nearly eighty-one years.

Another stone commemorates Reuben Bromley, a
successful sea captain who retired from the sea in
middle life to " actively engage in Christian and benevo-
lent effort for promoting the welfare of seamen."   He
was an officer of the Seamen's Bank for Savings from
its founding in 1829 to his death, and was also, it is
said, one of the founders of the Sailor's Snug Harbor
on Staten Island.

A plain dark monument in the Gardiner plot tells its own story in these words:

"David Gardiner, born May 29, 1784.
Died February 28, 1844."

"In the vigor of life, adorned by eminent virtues, solid abilities and rare accomplishments, beloved and venerated, he was stricken with instant death by the bursting of the great gun on board of the steam frigate Princeton in the River Potomac. A national calamity which wrung men's hearts and deprived the country of some of its most distinguished and valuable citizens."

His daughter, Julia, afterward married President John Tyler, and became the mother of several children, one of whom sleeps near his grandfather after crowding into his brief span of forty years such perils, hardships, vicissitudes, and misfortunes as few are called upon to undergo. His epitaph reads:

"Here lyeth John Alexander Tyler, son of John Tyler, President of the United States, and of Julia Gardiner, his wife, born at Sherwood Forest, James River, Virginia, April 7, 1848, died at Santa Fe, New Mexico, September 1, 1888."

"Alexander Tyler while a mere youth joined the fortunes of his native State, and became a member of the First Virginia Battalion of Artillery under General Robert Lee. Although enduring great privation and hardship, which he bore with uncomplaining fortitude, he served until the close of the Civil War, and was then paroled at Appomattox Court House in 1865. He went to Europe where he remained for eight years, first as a student at Carlsruhe, Baden, afterwards at Freiburg, Saxony, where he graduated as a mining and civil engineer. While at the latter place he entered the German army by special permit as a volunteer in the First Uhlan regiment under the command of Prince John of Saxony, and was actively engaged during the French and Prussian wars of 1870–71, receiving at the close a decoration from the hands of the Emperor William I, for gallant and distinguished services."

This gentleman, after serving with honor through two sanguinary wars, returned to his native country only to die suddenly of a fever contracted in New Mexico while performing the duties of his profession as a mining and civil engineer.

A mild literary interest attaches to a row of six or eight mossy headstones near the center of the yard, those of the Isaacs family, father, mother, brothers and sisters of John Howard Payne.

What might be called the wreck annals of the churchyard are interesting. Here lie the remains of those who perished in the off-shore whale fishery, which was prosecuted with vigor by the townsmen for years. "On February 24, 1719," we read, "a whaleboat being alone the men struck a whale, and she coming under the boat in passing, stoved it, and though ye men were not hurt with ye whale, yet before any help came to them four men tired and chilled and fell off ye boat and oars to which they hung and were drowned."

Here also repose the hundreds who have been wrecked upon this dangerous coast since commerce began in these waters nearly three hundred years ago.

CHAPTER XVII

THE WRECK OF THE JOHN MILTON

ALTHOUGH the Milton struck on Montauk, data of the tragedy can only be gained in the old churchyard of Easthampton, and in the village itself.[1] Entering the yard from the north, the first memorial introduces one of its peculiar offices — that of custodian of the ocean's trophies. This is a shaft of marble in the center of a large square mound, bearing this inscription:

"This stone was erected by individual subscriptions from various places to mark the spot where, with peculiar solemnity, were deposited the mortal remains of the three mates and eighteen of the crew of the ship, *John Milton*, of New Bedford, wrecked on the coast of Montauk, while returning from the Chincha Islands, on the 20th February, 1858, where, together with those who rest beneath, Ephraim Harding, the captain, and four others of the mariners, being the whole ship's company, were drowned in the waves. 'Thy way, O God, is in the sea.'"

After searching during three summers up and

[1] From *New York Evening Post*, 1890.

down the town, I succeeded in finding an old wrecker who had been first at the wreck of the *Milton*, who gave me a vivid account of it, and of the pathetic scenes attending the burial of the drowned seamen. "That was the worst wreck on the coast in later years," he began, "that of the *Milton*. She struck on a rock at Montauk, a quarter of a mile from shore, in a heavy snow storm. She was flying before a gale at the time and the shock was terrible. The vessel melted under it like a lump of sugar. I was one of the first on the spot. The shore looked like a wrecked shipyard. But for the breakers you could have walked for rods on the broken masts, spars, and timbers. There was the mainmast, four foot through, snapped off like a pipestem, every plank made into kindling wood, and every timber torn out of her. Only a part of the bow was left tossin' and crunchin' on the rock where she struck. The shock, you see, threw the anchors overboard and they held this fragment in place. But the sight of all was the dead bodies of the crew stretched out on the beach all frozen stiff, some covered with snow, or thrusting up a hand or arm above the drifts. Not a man was saved. One negro must have come ashore alive, for he had dragged himself some distance up the sands, but he had soon frozen. The ship's log-book came ashore, some trinkets and furniture, and that was all."

I did not need the words of my informant to picture

the excitement caused by this disaster through all the
eastern hamlets of the island. It was then much more
than now a maritime community. The large whaling
marine of Sag Harbor had been largely laid aside,
but the captains and crews who had manned it were
still living. Scores of wagons streamed out over
Montauk to the scene of the wreck, returning by twos
and threes, with the ghastly burdens which the sea had
relinquished. Then came the funeral. It is evident
from the impression made that no more solemn event
ever occurred in the village. The generous tars gathered
from far and near to perform the last sad rites to their
comrades. Bluff, hearty old sea captains, heroes of a
score of voyages, old salts tanned by the suns of every
clime, youngsters home from the first voyage, farmers,
merchants, sympathetic women, came from all the
Hamptons and all the Harbors — from Sagg and
Jericho, from Egypt, Pantago, the Springs, the Fireplace — as far west as to Quogue and the Manor,
quite filling the old church, about whose altar the
coffins had been disposed. They preserve old things
in Easthampton, and so I succeeded in finding the
sermon which the Rev. Stephen L. Mershon preached
on the occasion. His text was Job xxvii. 20, 21.
Then in the presence of the dead and the awestruck
living he enunciated these sentences:

"It is a solemn providence that has called us together.
We have come to pay our last tribute of respect to the

dead. But how unlike our usual assembling to cele-
brate these sad rites. It is not the member of our
community whose name has often sounded in our
ears; it is not the long-known friend, it is not the
relative, not the dear member of our domestic circle
that we have come to bury. No, we have come to bury
the stranger. No father, no mother, no wife, no sister
attends this burial to moisten the grave's cold earth
with their tears. . . . But strange as it may appear,
singular as are the circumstances that now surround
us, it must be admitted that truly does a peculiar
solemnity become this hour. Each one must feel that
God is speaking the language that tells of our mortality
in terms not to be mistaken. For it is not only one,
it is a congregation of the dead whom we now carry
to the grave. . . .

"In adverting to the circumstances that have called
us together let us not anticipate. On the morning of
December 6, 1856, we learn that the *John Milton* was
lying, a noble vessel of 1445 tons, in the harbor of New
York. That day was her broad canvas spread, that
like a winged bird of the ocean she might speed her
course to distant seas. . . . Five months from that
day her anchor was cast in the harbor of San Francisco.
Here, because of mutiny, thirteen of her crew were put
ashore, and as many more were shipped. But soon
again was the noble clipper released, and the day dawn
of August 10, 1857, brought them into the port of

Callao. Not long did she rest, for in about two weeks
we find her moored at the Chincha Islands. From
thence her course was homeward. On the 14th of the
present month (February) she anchored in Hampton
Roads, waiting orders from her owners. On the 16th,
but twelve short days since, the crew again spread the
canvas of their gallant vessel. With light and favorable breezes they put to sea, hoping soon to be in the
harbor of their home. Bright visions of home, of hap-
piness, of friends, were doubtless flitting across the
brain and playing sportively with them in their dreams.
Homeward they were bound. But no; a hand that
now lies powerless soon recorded, on the 17th, on
Wednesday morning, 'strong winds, double reef top-
sails, latter part strong winds and thick snow storm.'
From that hour they rode upon the sea where the storm-
king was in the ascendant. Dark and gloomy must
have been the nights that followed. All clouded was
the sky. They knew not where they were. No eye,
no glass could pierce the atmosphere; for on the morning of the 18th, on Thursday, the last entry but one in
the log-book tells us that strong gales are still prevailing and thick snow. The last entry is on that same
day: 'Latter part more moderate, and turned reefs
out'; when by observation they found themselves in
the latitude of 36 deg. 56 min. — in the exact latitude
of Cape May, at the southern extremity of the State
of New Jersey. . . .

"No longer have we any witness to tell their course, other than the gale that came with them upon the land. From Wednesday afternoon till Saturday we know that they rode upon the waves of the storm enveloped with falling snow. . . Friday was a day of terror. Such fear and terror were in the crew that the log-book was forgotten. The night that followed was the night of the landward tempest that burst upon our shore at the opening of day from the sea. Our ship was flying before its first and heaviest gale. The wind of that tempest was the east wind. By it they were carried away, by it they had departed from those deep channels of the ocean where the strong oak-timbered vessel could long have safely defied the fury of the gale. As the morning of Saturday opened upon them, and as all eyes were straining to catch some glimpses of the sun, the hand that moved in the storm hurled them upon the rocks of our shore. The work was done. It was but the deed of a moment. Masts, spars, sails, officers, and crew were all in one confused mass. The *John Milton* was no longer a monarch upon the sea. The ruins of her crown lay in wild confusion at the feet of her throne."

The bodies of the drowned were deposited in a common grave in the old churchyard here, and the people of the various towns contributed funds for the erection of this monument to their memory.

The above is only one of the many like tragedies

that the old churchyard covers. At the foot of the
shaft to the *Milton's* crew, on the west, are thirteen
grassy graves, all, save one, marked by wooden head-
boards. They cover the victims of the wreck of the
Circassian in 1877, not members of the ship's company, but of the wrecking crew who were engaged at
the time upon her, and who were overwhelmed with
the vessel by a sudden storm. There is a possible
romance in this group of graves. One of them is
distinguished from its companions by a fine marble
headstone which bears this description: "In loving
remembrance of Andrew Allan Nodder, æ. seventeen
years, son of Richard and Mary Nodder, of Wanstree,
near Liverpool, England. His young life was lost at
the wreck of the *Circassian*, December 29, 1877."
The dreamer among the graves is apt to query why
this son of wealthy well-born parents came to end his
life as a member of a coast-wrecking crew.[1]

[1] Nodder, we have since been informed, was an apprentice belong-
ing to the ship's crew.

CHAPTER XVIII

KING PHARAOH'S WIDOW

FROM the green hilltop where I write, July 25, 1882, can be seen across the downs two brown weather-beaten cottages, nestled at the base of a range of hills which skirt the blue line of the Sound. These cottages shelter eleven souls, the last remnants of the once proud tribe of Montaukett. In one dwells Queen Maria, widow of the last King, David Pharaoh, with her seven children, and in the other Charles Fowler, with his wife and child. Enter these dwellings and you find them bare and cheerless, with no carpets on the floor and only the rudest articles in the way of furniture. The inmates are idle, ignorant, dissipated, none of them pure Indian, there being a liberal intermixture of negro blood. They live from hand to mouth by hunting, fishing, doing odd jobs for the proprietor, and on the proceeds of a small interest in the land of the nature of a usufruct. Between Wyandanch, the first King of Montauk known to Europeans, and David Pharaoh, the last, a period of two hundred and fifty years intervened. The early history of the Montauketts has been told in the books and need not be dwelt on at

length here. They were the ruling tribe of Long
Island and dwelt in a fortified village on Montauk.
Wyandanch, their king, espoused the cause of the
English, and was for this reason hated by Ninicraft,
the powerful sachem of the Narragansetts, who declared war against him. About 1656 Ninicraft made
a descent on the Montauketts while they were cele-
brating the nuptials of the chief's daughter, burned
their villages, slew many of their people, and took
others captive. Two years later, in 1658, a great
pestilence carried off many of the remainder, and
Wyandanch was himself slain by poison administered
by a follower. This is no doubt familiar to the reader.

A subject little touched upon, however, is their later
history and the various efforts that were made, under
authority of the London Society for the Propagation
of the Christian Religion in New England, to educate
and Christianize them. The spiritual care of these
Indians was at first entrusted to the ministers of the
church at Easthampton, who met with little success
in their efforts. In 1741 the Society appointed the
Rev. Azariah Horton as a missionary to the Montauketts.
This devoted clergyman resided among them for several
years, learned their language to some extent, opened
schools, and was so successful that he led them to re-
nounce their idolatry and adopt the Christian religion.
After Mr. Horton's departure the Society pursued the
plan of sending teachers and preachers of their own

race among them. Several are mentioned in the records as having labored here with more or less success. By far the most distinguished was Sampson Occum, a member of the Mohegan tribe of Connecticut. Occum was born in 1723, and in his youth attracted the attention of Dr. Eleazer Wheelock, of Lebanon, who placed him at "Moor's Indian Charity-School" at Lebanon, an institution under the patronage of the Earl of Dartmouth, and which was later removed to Hanover and incorporated as Dartmouth College, where he received a good education and became a Christian. In 1755 Occum opened a school on Montauk, and preached and taught there until 1761. At this time the tribe numbered 182 souls. After him came several Indian teachers and preachers, the last, Paul Cuffee, a Shinnecock half-breed, acting as their spiritual teacher until a comparatively recent period. They also were cared for by the church at Easthampton during this period, Dr. Lyman Beecher, while pastor there, frequently riding across the wastes to preach to the Indians at Montauk. The result of these efforts was discouraging. A competent observer, the late Mr. David Gardiner, of East Hampton, thus epitomizes it: "Some of them learned to read and write, but their progress in knowledge neither ameliorated their condition, nor divested them of their natural improvidence. Their thirst for the liquid fire of the white man continued, with scarcely an exception, as ardent as when they first became acquainted with civilized life, and the domestic comforts of the hearth were little enhanced beyond the savage state, notwithstanding all the advantages of intercourse with a moral and religious people, disposed to treat them with sobriety and friendship. The efforts in this case for regenerating the Indian character were certainly a decided failure, and may be added to the thousand others which have disappointed the hopes of the philanthropist."

Not the least interesting feature of Montauk are the relics of this unfortunate people that still exist. On a high hill on the east side of Fort Pond Bay are the well-defined lines of a fort built by Wyandanch after the descent of the Narragansetts. It was about 100 feet square, with rampart and parapet of earth, a ditch at the foot of the glacis, and, tradition says, was palisaded — in all, a quite creditable piece of military engineering. About half a mile southeast there is an ancient Indian burial-ground, and near this the most celebrated of the relics of Montauk — a granite stone on whose smooth surface is the deep imprint of a human foot. Had some wandering Indian stepped upon the granite in a plastic state, the impression could not have been more perfect and distinct. Two other similar prints have been found on the plateau, and one has been removed, my informant thought, by some historical society. In all the heel of the foot is toward the east and the toes to the west — prophetic, perhaps, of the westward march of the poor Indian. There is no legend current as to their origin except the one mentioned below, that they were made by the foot of the evil spirit in his flight. The Indians held them in superstitious awe, and frequent pow-wows were held in their vicinity. Another curious stone is encountered as one enters upon Montauk — a granite rock, smooth and flat, upon which are several red marks as of blood. The Indian legend says that they were made by the blood of a chief who was killed there by an enemy's arrow. One frequently meets little cavities in the ground in his rambles, which were once deep pits where Indian corn was stored. In the old records these are called "Indian barns." In high places on the north shore, where the wind has removed the sand, chippings of white flint mark the site of Indian workshops where arrows, spears, and tomahawks were chipped into form. Heaps of shells still mark their ancient feasting places, and their weapons and domestic utensils are quite frequently picked up on the shores of Fort Pond and Great Pond. Perhaps the most thrilling legend that haunts Montauk is that of the raising of Mutcheshesumetook, the Evil One. The great event of the Indian year was the stranding of a whale on the beach. Its flesh furnished food, its oil light, its hide thongs, its bones points for weapons, and its tail or fin, roasted in the fire, was the most acceptable offering that could be made to Saw-wonnuntoh, their deity. The sacrifice was offered amid the whole concourse of the people, with feasts, dances, yells, and incantations on the part of the medicine-men to drive off the Evil One, who was also known to regard it as a choice tid-bit. Now, it so happened that at one of these pow-wows the incantations were so powerful that Mutcheshesumetook appeared in visible form and was pursued westward by the whole body of people. In his flight he stepped on the granite rock of which I have spoken, and left the impress of his foot, which time cannot efface.

CHAPTER XIX

AN ISLAND MANOR

NEARLY opposite Easthampton at the entrance to the Sound lies a small island as peculiar in its social and political history as in its physical conformation. It is known as Gardiner's Island. Once it was a long tongue of land jutting out from the main body of the island, but the strong currents of the Atlantic have eaten away the connecting portion, leaving an oval-shaped mass of gravelly hills and dales, some seven miles in circumference and containing some thirty-three hundred acres. Its history is curious. Lion Gardiner, a soldier of fortune from the Low Countries, bought it of the Indian owners in 1639. Shortly afterward he received a patent of it from Lord Stirling, for which he paid " a little more," and agreed to give a yearly annuity of five pounds, if demanded. In 1640 he removed to the island with his young wife and child, and, dying in 1663, bequeathed it to his eldest son, and this example being followed by those who succeeded him, the estate has remained in the family name unbroken for ten generations.[1]

[1] 1885.

The Gardiner Mansion, Gardiner's Island

The social order on the island is quite patriarchal.
The proprietor is the social and political head of the
domain. Though grazing is the chief business of the
estate, large quantities of hay, grain, and roots are
raised, and this necessitates the employment of some
thirty farm hands, nearly all of whom were born on
the island. Some have grown gray in the service
without ever having left the island except for brief
visits to the mainland. Many have married there,
and have families of their own, so that there is a little
community of between fifty and sixty souls for whom
the proprietor must provide food, clothing, shelter,
school, and chapel.

A personal visit to the island is attended with some
difficulty. The nearest point on the Long Island
shore is a sand pit, known as "The Fireplace," some
four miles distant. The nearest settlement is "The
Springs," a little hamlet of two stores, a post-office,
and several weather-beaten houses. Boats from the
island generally come to this place every Saturday for
supplies, and if one has the proper credentials he may
secure a passage on their return trip and will be sure
of a welcome at his journey's end. There is no harbor
on the island, the boats landing on the western shore
at a little boathouse built high up on the open beach
for their protection. From this point a gravelly path
winds through open grounds to the mansion house
of the estate, perhaps an eighth of a mile inland. This

is a long, roomy country seat, painted white, with wide gables and dormer windows, a deep porch in front extending the whole length of the building, and is shaded by fine old forest trees. The present structure only dates back to a few years before the Revolution, but in its treasures of relics and priceless heirlooms it is surpassed by none. In the library are more hunting trophies, some rare old books and documents, land grants, patents, commissions, and the like, on paper and parchment discolored with age. One of the rare books is the family Bible of Lion Gardiner, in which is inscribed in his own hand this quaint bit of history:

"In the year of our Lord 1635, July 10, came I, Lion Gardiner, and Mary, my wife, from Woredon, a town in Holland, where my wife was born, being daughter of one Dirike Wilamson. . . . We came from Woredon to London and thence to New England, and dwelt at Saybrook fort four years, of which I was Commander, and there was born unto me a son named David in 1636, April the 29th, the first born in that place, and in 1638 a daughter was born called Mary, August the 30th, and then I went to an island of mine own which I bought of the Indians, called by them Manchonoke and by me Isle of Wight, and there was born another daughter named Elizabeth, Sept. 14, 1641, she being the first child born there of English parents."

Rare old china and bric-à-brac, glossy perukes,

wonderful frills, and dainty silken robes odorous of camphor and lavender, are only a few of the treasured relics which the old mansion boasts. Among them was until recently a diamond from Captain Kidd's stores, and a cradle quilt of cloth of gold presented by that freebooter to the wife of the third proprietor in return for a dinner of roast pig at which he was a self-invited guest. Contiguous to the house is a fine garden, and beyond it a dairy house, an old-fashioned windmill propelled by sails for grinding grain, several barns, cottages for the workmen, and a race-course for training blooded colts, the raising of which has become of late a leading industry on the farm.

One September morning, mounted on a spirited steed, I set out for an unrestricted gallop over the island. Turning into a rough wagon road leading southward, I cantered along past the race-course, green meadows, and yellow cornfields, and fields where the brood mares and their foals were quietly feeding, through several bars and gates, and at last emerged on the wide sheep pastures that occupy the entire southern portion of the island. Nearly a thousand acres in area, these pastures present every variety of landscape — steep bluffs, scarred hills, wide downs gay with golden-rod, little green hollows, patches of deep wood, marshes, and sea beaches. Some twenty-five hundred white, fleecy innocents were cropping the tender grass here, and at sight of the horseman scampered toward

him with a chorus of "baas," so that he was soon
surrounded by hundreds of the pretty creatures all
eager for the salt that is liberally showered upon them
by the herdsman in his visits. He had none, to his
sorrow, and, unable to withstand their appealing
glances, spurred his horse to the top of the highest
bluff on the eastern shore for a glance at his surroundings. From this point one looks out over the entire
island upon a weird, strange scene — a mass of tumbled
hills, gray downs, and delightful little hollows, much
resembling in some features the neighboring peninsula
of Montauk, although, unlike that, it supports here
and there patches of deep forest. At our feet the
Atlantic thundered. Northward we could see the gray
coastline of Connecticut; westward the hills sloped
gently down to the mansion house two miles away,
and on the south, stretching far out to sea, was the
long tongue of land known as Montauk, with the white
tower of the lighthouse marking its eastern extremity.
The cattle pastures, equal in extent to the sheep range,
occupy the northern side of the island, and are separated from the latter by fences of rail or stones. They
are capable of carrying a herd of four hundred head.
Leaving the shore, I went for a gallop inland through
these wastes. My horse leaped the watercourses and
tussocks, curved round the little circular pond holes
that dot the island, and threaded the patches of
forest with the skill of an old campaigner. Occasion-

ally we were met by a wild steer, in the wood we startled whole colonies of crows, that circled above us with vociferous cawings, and on every dry tree of any size was perched an immense fishhawk's nest, seemingly placed with an eye to the picturesque. An unwritten law severe as Draco's protects these birds on the island, and they are comparatively tame. No more favorable place for a study of their habits could be found. I learned from an old gray-haired workman, evidently a keen observer of nature, that they invariably leave the island on the same day in autumn — the 20th of October — and return as regularly on the 20th of May. Their nests are great conglomerations of sticks, straw, mud, and fish bones, fully six feet in diameter, and ludicrously large compared with the size of the bird. Their dexterity in taking their prey is something wonderful. My friend the laborer assured me that he had often seen them strike flatfish, proverbially quick of movement, eleven feet beneath the surface, and bear them in triumph to their nests. On my return after completing the circuit of the island I passed the cemetery of the estate, a lonely little place of graves, separated from the waste by a fence of white palings, and with a great boulder in the center covered with a thick growth of vines. Here the several proprietors of the island are laid, except one, who died and was buried at Hartford.

One might make a chapter of the wild tales and

traditions of Kidd and his doings that haunt the island. Gardiner's Bay and its shores are said to have been a favorite resort of the pirate and others of his ilk. I saw the identical spot — on the border of a dense swamp in what was then a thick wood — where he buried the famous chest of treasure referred to by our friend, and heard many tales of pirate daring and enormities. Kidd often came to the mansion house in the days of the third proprietor, was a self-invited guest at his table, and took forcibly such provisions as his ships needed, although he always paid prodigally for them. The reputation of the island as a depository of hidden treasure was for a long time a source of annoyance to the owners from the hordes of treasure-seekers that it attracted thither, but the guild has now become nearly extinct.

CHAPTER XX

THE WHALEMEN OF SAG HARBOR

IN 1845 Sag Harbor had a population of 2700 souls; the last census gives it but 1996.[1] The grand list of the town shows a more startling decrease, all attributable to the loss of the whaling interest, which forty years ago lined its docks with ships and made the town a familiar name in every Old World port, and in the islands of the sea as well. This decadence is made more manifest by a stroll through the village. You walk through streets where a slumberous quiet prevails, and whose dust rests undisturbed by traffic. You pass fine old country seats gained by adventurous voyages in the Atlantic and Pacific, from the Arctic to the Antarctic, but whose occupants are rarely to be tempted now from their snug harborage. Along the water front are ruins of oil-cellar, warehouse, cooper-shop and sail-loft, covering acres; two or three old hulks, foundered and rotting on the shallows, and a long dock, untenanted save by fishing smacks, with perhaps two or three old whalemen lounging listlessly

[1] This figure has increased considerably since 1882, the time this was written.

upon it, and a single cart loading with cordwood, sole representative of the hurry and bustle that once characterized it. To gain a vivid idea of the town at its best estate, however, one must win the confidence of one of the old ship captains who still remain snugly moored in the port, or, better still, get an interview with some member of the old shipping firms, who once had their score of vessels out in as many seas, and handled products to the value of millions annually. In his former shipping-office, I met recently a gentleman of the latter class, who favored me not only with many interesting facts concerning the prosecution of the business in former days, but with much agreeable reminiscence besides. The shipping-office was in itself a study; a small room, with bare floors, fitted with a stove, desk, armchairs, and a quaint old secretary, in which was stored a variety of books and documents — ledgers filled with long columns of figures, musty log-books, records of long-forgotten voyages, invoices, manifests, clearances, contracts, advances, outfits, leases of vessels, and the like, with samples of oil, whaling relics, and curiosities from foreign climes. Quite frequently during the conversation my informant refreshed his memory by a reference to this store of documents.

It is a fact not generally known, perhaps, that the first vessel to make a long-distance whaling voyage sailed from Sag Harbor. She was gone but a few

months, running down into the South Atlantic, and
returned unsuccessful. Nothing daunted, her owners
fitted out other vessels, which returned with full holds,
netting them a handsome profit. New London,
Stonington, New Bedford, and Nantucket — all nearly
opposite — were quick to perceive the possibilities of
the whale fishery assured by this successful voyage,
and engaged in the business with ardor. The palmy
days of the town and of the whaling industry culminated in 1845. At this time the village had sixty-
four ships scattered over the globe in pursuit of whales;
and my informant had counted as many as fourteen
ships lying in the harbor at one time waiting to unload
cargo. He gave a vivid picture of the "high days"
witnessed in the village then. Ships lay three abreast
at the long dock. Eight hundred riggers, coopers,
sailmakers, and stevedores went on and off the wharves
daily. Thousands of barrels of oil lay in the oil
cellars, piled tier above tier and covered with seaweed.
Great warehouses, three stories high, the upper stories
filled with whalebone and spermaceti, the lower used
as sail and rigging lofts, alternated along the water
front with rows of long cooper shops. Lighters were
coming and going from the ships in the bay, hundreds
of carts moving oil and bone from the docks, the adze
of the cooper and hammer of blacksmith and outfitter
rang all day long, and the streets were filled with
crews of outgoing or incoming vessels, attended by

their wives, daughters, and sweethearts, mingling welcomes and farewells, weeping and laughter. Four firms in the village at this time were among the heaviest owners in the trade — Howell Brothers & Hunting, Mulford & Slate, Charles T. Deering, and H. & S. French. The majority of the ships, however, were owned by a number of stockholders who formed regularly organized companies.

The vessels employed were rarely new, more often packet ships whose defective sailing qualities unfitted them for passenger traffic, or old craft that had outlived their usefulness. Of the latter class some notable vessels came into the hands of the shipmasters, among them the *Thames*, famous in missionary annals, and the *Cadmus*, the ship that brought Lafayette to this country in 1824. These were purchased or leased by the shipping firms, refitted, and sent out on voyages of from one to three years' duration. Whaling cruises were at first limited to the North and South Atlantic, but as the whales became less and less plentiful there, they were extended until they embraced the entire circuit of the globe. A favorite three years' voyage in 1845 was to the Azores, thence to St. Helena, and down the West Coast, around the Cape of Good Hope, through the Indian Ocean to Australia, thence to the North Pacific, thence south through the Polynesian Islands, around Cape Horn and home.

It was no light matter to fit out a vessel for one of

these voyages. The sails, running rigging, cables, and boats were inspected with the utmost care. From a paper containing instructions to the outfitter of the bark *Pacific*, bound on a three years' voyage, I find he was to "have yards all up to topmast heads, spare spars, if any, on deck, jib-boom rigged in, anchors on bows, both chains on deck and forward to windlass, or between windlass and bow; rigging all overhauled, mizzen rigging all new, including backstays; all head rigging new, also fore topmast and topgallant stays." This done, a crew of twenty-two picked men was to be provided, with three boats and their complement of harpoons, lances, lines, and hatchets, together with 2000 or 3000 well-seasoned barrels and a great variety of provisions and miscellaneous stores. A little book containing the list of articles furnished the bark *Pacific* above mentioned in 1852 lies before me, and to satisfy the reader's curiosity I subjoin a list of the most important. Under the head of provisions and cabin stores were: 1 barrel kiln-dried meal, 500 pounds pork hams, 100 gallons vinegar, 2 quintals codfish, 500 pounds sugar, 400 pounds coffee, 400 pounds dried apples, 2 boxes raisins, 30 barrels beans, 20 bushels corn, 100 bushels potatoes, 200 gallons lamp oil, 1 box sperm candles, 3 boxes hard soap, $1\frac{1}{2}$ chests of tea, 50 pounds crushed sugar, 6 pounds mustard, 25 pounds black pepper, 20 pounds ginger, 28 pounds spices, 30 pounds saleratus, 1 box pepper sauce, 3 bags table salt,

6 packages preserved meats. In her medicine chest she carried 1 case Holland gin, 1 gallon brandy, 1 of port wine, and 10 of whiskey. Under the head of "miscellaneous" articles were tar, 20 cords of oak wood, chains, head straps, old junk, white oak butts, boat knees, stems and timbers, 15 pounds sand, 1 cask sawdust, 1 cask lime, 3 whaling guns, 50 bomb lances, lance powder, 1 spun yarn winch, and 1 mincing machine. As "ship chandlery" she carried scrubbing brushes, chopping knives, lamp wicks, coffee mills, Bristol brick, sieves, 4 sets knives, beeswax, tacks, brass and iron screws, shovels, hoes, rigging leather, pump leather, matches, and ensigns, 29 varieties of cooper's tools, and quite an assortment of crockery and tinware. Under the head of "cordage" there were 20 manila lines, 2 tarred, 1 coil lance line, 1 coil mar-line, 4 coils spun yarn, 12 coils ratlines, ropes for jib-stay, and 8 coils manilla rope. Under head of "slops," tobacco, reefing jackets, duck trousers, and denims, Guernsey frocks, twilled kersey shirts, tarpaulin hats, southwesters, mounted palms, shoes, and brogans are enumerated.

Captain, mates, and seamen all sailed on the "lay," that is, for a certain percentage of the cargo secured. This percentage varied with the different owners and captains. Usually a captain received one sixteenth, a mate one twenty-fourth, a boat-steerer one ninetieth, and ordinary seamen one one-hundred-and-tenth of the

catch. The remainder fell to the owners, who bore
all the expenses of the voyage. This system gave
every man an interest in securing a "big lay," and
worked admirably. An outcome of this plan, which
entailed no end of loss and vexation on the owners, was
the system of "advances," by which they advanced
to the men tobacco, clothes, and money, often
to the full value of their share in the prospective
cargo.

The return of a vessel from a three years' voyage
was an event in the village. Keen eyes were generally
on the watch, and as soon as she was sighted a pilot-
boat, filled with the owners and friends of the ship's
officers, sailed down the harbor to welcome her. Meanwhile news of the arrival spread through the village,
and with marvelous rapidity to the outlying hamlets,
Bridgehampton, Easthampton, etc., whence the crews
were largely recruited, and as the vessel drew up to the
dock a throng of friends and relatives of the crew
were gathered to greet them. The scene that ensued
may be imagined; it was not without its more somber
aspects, however, for often it could only be said of
some one that he had been crushed in the whale's
jaws, or by a fall from the masthead, or had perished
of fever and been buried on some island of the sea.
The men ashore, the owners and skipper made an
inspection of the cargo; vials were filled with samples
of oil to be forwarded to the commission houses in New

York through whom the cargo was sold, and the vessel was ordered unloaded.

Traditions of wonderfully lucrative voyages made by some of these vessels still linger in the port. The *Thomas Jefferson*, after a year's voyage, returned with $132,000 worth of oil and bone. She cost her owners $17,000, and netted them that year $40,000. The ship *Hudson*, absent from her dock just seven months, thirteen and one-half days, without sighting land in the interim, brought back 2400 barrels of oil. The ship *Cadmus* made as good a voyage. The bark *Pacific* was most unfortunate at first. At Pernambuco, on her first voyage, she lost her captain, and was obliged to return. On a second venture to the Pacific she was dismasted by a typhoon, and again returned empty. On her third voyage she netted her owners $7000. Loss and risk were incident to the business, however, as in the case of the ship *Flying Cloud*, owned in Sag Harbor, but sent to New Bedford with a full cargo for a market. There her owners were offered seventy-two cents per gallon for their oil, but preferred to ship it to England, where they secured, after nearly a year's delay, twenty-six cents per gallon.

I was curious to learn the cause for the decline of this once lucrative business, and was surprised to find it attributed almost solely to the California excitement of 1849. Whalemen, from their life of adventure, were at once attracted by tales of the richness of the new

El Dorado, and removed thither by hundreds.   Whole
crews deserted from whale ships lying in San Francisco,
and made for the diggings, so that, with none to man
them, the vessels were laid up at the wharfs.   A great
fire in 1845, which destroyed docks, warehouses, and
other appliances, also contributed to this end.

CHAPTER XXI

THE best story-teller at Southampton one season years ago was a little old man in saffron-colored nankeens such as the beaux of fifty years ago were wont to wear. He rarely lacked an audience, and many a strange yarn he spun with quaint earnestness that seemed to bolster up the weak points in the story with strange effect.

"This beach is the real treasure island, don't you know," he said, one day as he sat on the shore and waved his hand out to the shining stretch of sand. "Not only has it received the wrecks of the great fleets, entering the bay of the Western metropolis for nearly three hundred years, but it was Captain Kidd's great bank of deposit, as well as that of his illustrious compeers. Wedges of gold, great anchors, heaps of pearls, inestimable stones and pretty much everything else poor Clarence saw are here if only one knew where to look. If I have not dug and handled some of Kidd's treasure myself I have seen and handled the gross integument which once incased it; and as my previous tales have been legendary — although having the stamp of truth — in this case I can produce the ancient record itself. I was rummaging in a south side garret recently and there found an iron pot of peculiar shape, more 'pot bellied,' if you will excuse the term, and much heavier than those now in use, covered with a deep coat of rust.

"'Ah,' said my hostess, when I reported the find, 'that is the Captain Kidd pot. It was dug up yonder by my grandfather over a hundred years ago. Here is a paper,' she added, 'that will tell you all about it.'

"It was a very old paper, indeed, yellow with time, and almost ready to fall to pieces, dated 'New London, Connecticut, June 28, 1790,' but the name had been torn or had fallen off, to my vexation. However, she pointed to a letter from a correspondent in Southampton which read as follows: 'Yesterday a young man in this place dug up a stone and a pot under it full of dollars. He called in his neighbors and digging deeper they found another and much larger pot. The stone and inscription I have seen. It appears to be a ballast stone. The engraving on it is much blurred. We think it was buried by Kidd. It was dug up within a quarter of a mile of our south shore, on a flat piece of land. The engraver must have been illiterate and the inscription cannot be imitated by printed types.'

"My hostess did not remember how many dollars were in the pot, but thought the sum a comfortable one. Not long afterward, in a garret in Easthampton,

I discovered Captain Kidd's old treasure chest, a heavy oaken box with great brass clasps and locks, that bore great store of precious stones, silver bars and cloth of gold when it was dug up on Gardiner's Island by order of the commissioners sent there by the royal governor for this special purpose. Kidd was on trial in Boston at the time for his crimes and told where he had buried several chests of treasure on Gardiner's Island in the hope of purchasing pardon. He was sent to England, however, tried and hanged in chains at Newgate. The woman who owned the chest was a descendant of the Gardiners of Gardiner's Island, and vouched for its genuineness as the treasure chest of Captain Kidd.

"But really, the greatest find ever made on this beach was that of my young friend and relative, Jack Belyea. Jack didn't say much about it for obvious reasons. He was here five summers ago. A shy, sensitive fellow naturally, but his great trouble that summer rendered him more so. You see, he wanted to marry Bertha, and Bertha confided to me that she was awfully in love with Jack, but unfortunately his bank account wasn't at all satisfactory to her parents and they forbade the union. So Jack had but a sorry summer of it, paced the sands revolving plans for increasing his worldly gear, and was often tempted to end it all by one plunge into the breakers. In one of these evil moments his foot struck a little ball of yarn, as he thought, and sent it spinning along the beach before him. Then, because he felt a spite against everything animate and inanimate, I suppose, he began kicking it on before him like a football. Presently he saw something strange about it and picked it up to examine it more closely. It was woven instead of wound, in a very curious and intricate way. Jack said this aroused his curiosity and, taking out his knife, he cut one by one the strands of strong Indian hemp of which it was composed. The last layer disclosed one of those horribly ugly and grotesque Indian idols, with which travelers to the Orient are familiar. One feature of it struck Jack as very unusual — its stomach was very large and protruded in an unnatural way. A few strokes of his knife opened it when, lo, out fell six of the largest and most beautiful diamonds ever seen outside of kings' regalia.

"How they rolled and sparkled on the hard sand! Jack stood dazed for a moment, then scrambled to pick them up and hide them in his pocket. After this he peered farther into the cavity whence they came and found there a coiled ribbon of rice paper on which was written in Hindustan:

"'The gems have been my curse, therefore commit I them to the sea. Whosoever thou be that findest, keep not, but sell; if rich, give to the poor: if poor, enjoy thy wealth and give Allah thanks.'

"When Jack took his bank book to Bertha's father

a month later, the old gentleman was vastly surprised but could not gainsay the figures. He could only murmur a blessing. So Jack and Bertha were married."

Another day when we had gathered round the little old man at the base of Sand Hill Crane dune, he told this strange story of Captain Topping:

"I stood here last Michaelmas toward sunset watching the top hamper of a big East Indiaman sink beneath the waves, when suddenly a shadow enveloped me, cool, like a cloud, and looking up I beheld an odd figure a few yards off — a man of giant frame, leaning on an eel spear and regarding me not unkindly. His costume, sou'wester, pea jacket and heavy sea boots, bespoke the seafaring man of an earlier day, and his skin was so tanned and wrinkled by time and exposure that it hung in folds about his shrewd face and twinkling black eyes.

"As I looked up he turned his head in a listening attitude and then cried with startling energy: 'Fourth squadron, ahoy! ahoy!' There was no response, however, and after peering up and down the sands he turned to me.

"'Methought I heard our old cry — the weft! the weft! But I see it not. Old eyes are dim and old ears dull I find.'

"The weft; ah, yes, I remembered; the fisher's coat waved from a staff on the dunes, the signal to the whaling crews two hundred years ago that a whale was off shore — and then looking more closely I perceived that it was not an eel spear but a harpoon, that my strange visitor leaned upon.

"'And this is ——?' I queried.

"'Cap'n Thomas Topping at your service,' he replied with dignity.

"The name startled me. I had been nosing through the old records in the town clerk's office and recognized the name as that of one of the leading spirits in the settlement of the town, a famous Indian fighter and captain of the whaling crew, withal an ancestor of mine several generations back. I could only stare at him in wide mouthed wonder.

"'I've come back,' he continued in a thin, cracked, quavering voice, 'to see what these moderns are a doin', an' I confess I don't altogether admire the goin's on, I vow I can't fathom 'em. The place is far prettier than in my day. Oceans o' money must have been spent on the houses, lawns an' gardens, to say nothin' of the houses, kerridges and sich, but, fer all that, life ain't as well worth livin' here as it was in my day leastways not ter me.

"'Fust place I visited was my old windmill on Fortune Hill that Cap'n Eben Parsons leased of me an' run for nigh fifty year. Ef you had all the grain Cap'n Eben has seen run through them hoppers o' his, you'd be richer than you are, or like to be. Well,

the old mill was there just the same outwardly to
appearance, but inside — why, I found on openin'
the door and walkin' in that two likely lookin' wimmen
from Boston, or up that way, had bought it an' turned
it into a dwellin' hus. Think of livin' in a windmill;
an' they had fitted it up inside with all sort o' city
knicknacks an' furnishens, an' I must say had every-
thin' as snug an' cozy as could be.

"'I introduced myself as Cap'n Eben, who was
runnin' the mill when their fathers and mothers was
children, an' they appeared real glad to see me, asked
me to stay to tea. Naturally we fell to talkin' 'bout
their takin' up with an old mill fer a house. I tole 'em
that when Cap'n Eben an' Sabella Hand that was
a sparkin', arter they was promised, Cap'n Eben
wanted to be jined to onct, an' go to housekeepin' on
the ground floor o' his old mill, not bein' forehanded
enough to provide a house; but Sabella turned up her
nose at the idee; she said she guessed she wan't goin'
to be married to live in a mill; an' she waited six years
afore Cap'n Eben could provide a house to her notion.
The women marveled at Sabella's conduct, said they
didn't admire it a bit; for their part they delighted to
live in the old mill; and they asked me a heap o' questions — how I ground corn and wheat, and if the rats
and mice was so bold an' numerous then, and if the
wind moaned so ghost like through the vans o' nights
when a storm was brewin'.

"'I next went a lookin' fer the old meetin' house where Parson Hunting preached the pure gospel for goin' on fifty years; but dear me, there was a billiard room and bowling alley on the site; an' out where the horse sheds stood there was a space rolled smooth and young men and women in parti-colored raiment was a batting balls agin a net in the center. There was a woman on the stoop of a fine new house across the way watchin' em, an' I made bold to ask her where the meetin' 'us was moved to.

"'Law,' says she, 'you're a stranger here I guess. They moved it down agin the sand hills yonder, an' made a bran new buildin' of it, an' brought up a sextant from New York to take care of it.'

"'I was meandering peacefully down the street in search of the meetin' 'us, when of a suddint somethin' shot by me with a swish, a cretur like a man balanced on a frame hung between two wheels placed tandem — but what kept the thing up I couldn't see unless it was the power of the evil one. I thought it was one of them winged creturs, or wheels within wheels foretold by the prophet Elijah for the last days, an' I asked a boy if it was, and he said, "It's a bysickle, you old fool."

"'In my day children were taught to respect their elders.

"'The sextant took great pride in his meeting 'us an' showed me all over it.   It was a queer, low, mouse

like building, with a many towers and ells and angles
and no steeple, and was built mostly of wreck timber
gathered on the beach — so different from the stately
churches of my day with lofty steeples and pillared
porticos. I asked the sexton why they changed.
"Well," sez he, "they wanted somethin' different.
Them old-fashioned meetin' houses with tall steeples
an' four pillars in front was so familiar an' commonplace, they got to be an eyesore, so our trustees told
the architect to git 'em up somethin' novel an' un-
heard of. An' he done it."

"'The fact is,' said the old warrior, slightly chang-
ing his position, 'I don't understand these moderns. They cum here an' build houses, costin' fifty
thousan' dollars apiece — that would a bought the
hull township in my day, includin' the whalin' outfit — an' only occupy 'em tew or three months in
the year, or not at all. An' then the trumpery! they
fill 'em up with spinnin' wheels, hatchets, and old
irons, trammels, arm cheers, pots and kittles; what
we used they keep for ornaments. I hed ter laugh
when I see at one place Deacon 'Siah Howell's ole
arm cheer of English oak he bro't with him from
Suffolk a standin' on the front stoop, tied all over
with blue ribbons.'

"While speaking, my strange visitor had kept his
weather eye to seaward and his huge fingers gripped
the harpoon staff.

"Suddenly there came a distant cry: 'The weft! The weft! Weft! Weft!'

"'There she blows! There she blows!' and with a shout of glee my venerable ancestor made off amid the sand hills and I never saw him again."

CHAPTER XXII

THE SHINNECOCKS[1]

A MILE and a half from Southampton lie the wide reservation and rude dwellings of the Shinnecock Indians — with the possible exception of the Mashpees on Cape Cod, the most numerous and respectable of existing Eastern tribes. One finds their history and the story of their connection with the whites, as contained in the quaint old Southampton records, exceedingly interesting. When the first settlers of Southampton came here from Massachusetts in 1640, they were, next to the Montaukets, the dominant tribe on the island, with a territory extending from Canoe Place on the west to Easthampton on the east, including the whole south shore of Peconic Bay, and their warriors, according to tradition, reaching when arranged in Indian file from "Shinnecock gate to the town" — about two miles — and numbering 2000 men.

Southampton was purchased of the Shinnecocks.

---

[1] Written for the *Evening Post* in 1886. The Shinnecocks still retain their tribal autonomy and reservation and have about held their own in numbers, but it is said there is scarcely a full-blood Shinnecock among them.

The deed is still preserved in the town records, an instrument dating back to 1640, and setting forth, in the old terminology, that Pomatuck, Manduck, and seven others, "native Indians and true owners of the eastern part of Long Island, for the consideration of sixteen coats and threescore bushels of corn, and in further consideration that the English should defend the said Indians from the unjust violence of whatever Indians should illegally assail them," conveyed to the whites "the lands commonly known by the name of the place where the Indians bayle over their canoes out of the North Bay (Peconic) to the south side of the island, all the lands lying eastward of that point." The purchase also included all the planted land "eastward from the first creek at the westermore end of Shinnecock plain." For more than sixty years Indian and white continued to dwell in the greatest harmony — the energies of the former, as their hunting privileges grew less, being absorbed in the off-shore whale fishery. Some curious entries in the town records pertaining to this matter are interesting as showing the relations existing between the parties. In 1670 Paquanang and other Indians agreed with a Southampton company "to whale for the next three years the same way as the last three years, and in addition a pot such as John Cooper gives his Indians." By an instrument of 1671 Atingquoin agreed to whale for the next season "for one coat before it commenced, one when the season was half over, and a third when it ended," or "for a pot, a pair of shoes and stockings, one-half of a pound of powder, and three pounds of shot." In other cases they were employed in trying out the blubber, for a certain share in the oil. By 1703, however, their hunting lands had nearly all slipped away, and they became restless and dissatisfied, whereupon a grand convention of whites and Indians was held at Southampton and the matter amicably settled, the town giving the Indians a lease of Shinnecock Hills at a nominal rental of one ear of corn, paid annually — the meadows, marshes, grass, herbage, feeding, pasturage, timber, stone, and convenient highways excepted; the Indians, however, to have the privilege of ploughing and planting certain portions of it. They were also given liberty to cut flags, bulrushes, and such grass as they made their baskets of, and to dig ground-nuts, "mowing lands excepted."

Shinnecock Hills is the beautiful tract of rolling country, comprising pastures only, occupying the narrow neck between Peconic and Shinnecock Bays. It was held by the Indians under the lease of 1703 until 1859, when, by special act of the Legislature, they conveyed their right in it to the proprietors of Southampampton, receiving in return the fee of their present reservation on Shinnecock Neck. The proprietors continued to hold the hills in common until 1861, when they were sold at public auction for $6250, the purchasers being a company of Southampton farmers, who proposed to hold it for grazing purposes, as had been done for centuries by their ancestors. The tract has recently been purchased by a company of Brooklyn capitalists, who propose, it is said, converting it into a summer resort. Since the exchange the Indians have continued to reside quietly on their reservation of some 600 acres on Shinnecock Neck. The writer's visit to them was in company with Mr. Edward Foster, of Southampton, one of the editors of its records, and a gentleman well versed in the affairs of the Indians. We drove into the country perhaps a mile beyond the last of the straggling village houses, and at the foot of a little depression in the plain crossed a brook just where it fell into an arm of Shinnecock Bay. On the left, curving around the shore of the bay, and bounded on the west by a similar arm, with Shinnecock Hills beyond, lay a wide plain, burdened near us with growing corn and wheat, but showing further in the rear untilled fields covered with weeds and brush, groves of forest trees, and, scattered here and there, a score of brown, mossy, one-story cottages. This was the reservation. We drove through the corn-fields, past the cottages to the south end, and returned along the western shore, making the circuit of the tract.

"Very few of the Indians till their lands," remarked my companion; "they are let out by the trustees to outside parties. The government of the reservation is a little peculiar. It is vested entirely in three trustees, members of the community, who are elected annually by the tribe in the room where our town meetings are held. These men, with the consent of three of our justices of the peace, have full power over the land on the reservation. They cannot sell it, for it is held only in fee; but they can lease it for a limited period, not exceeding three years, and then perform the ordinary duties of overseers. The land is excellent, giving good crops of wheat and corn, as good as any in this vicinity, but two thirds of it is gone to waste through the in-dolence of the Indians in not cultivating it. There are some twenty-five houses on the reservation, which, allowing five persons to each house, would give a total of 125 inhabitants; but probably not two thirds of the tribe remain at home, the others leading a roving ex-istence — whaling, fishing, wrecking, and as farm laborers. They have a good school, kept by a colored master, two churches — Congregational and Millerite — but no resident pastor, the office being filled some-times by the Presbyterian minister at Southampton, sometimes by itinerant clergy, and again by members of the Young Men's Christian Association."[1]

By this time we had passed several cottages, and

[1] What was the Congregational Church or body has now been taken under the care of the Long Island Presbytery and a resident minister is supplied by the Presbyterian Church and its friends. The Millerite Church still lacks a resident pastor.

had arrived at one which bore a neater, more inviting appearance than its neighbors.

"This was the former home of Priest Lee," remarked my friend, "father of a somewhat remarkable family, and a characteristic one. He is dead, but Mrs. Lee is living. Suppose we call."

As we drew up before the open doorway an elderly woman, tall, straight, showing strong traces of Indian blood, came and framed herself in the doorway.

"We wished to ask about your husband," said my companion. "He was a colored man, I think, a native of Maryland?"

"Yes," she replied.

"And you have had five sons, every one a seaman, and several rising to be masters?"

"Yes, sir."

"My friend would like to hear about the boys, some of their exploits, the ships they sailed in, and the like."

Here the old lady hesitated. Her memory was too poor, she said: "But there is Garrison in the truck patch," she continued, brightening; "he could tell you all about it." Garrison was the youngest son, a stalwart fellow of over six feet, showing the Indian characteristics as plainly as his mother; and leaning on his plough handles, he gave us his family annals modestly, but without hesitation.

"There were five brothers of us," he began — "Milton, Ferdinand, Notely, Robert, and myself,

William Garrison. Milton went to sea young, followed whaling sixteen or seventeen years, and died. Ferdinand rose to be mate, and then captain of the ship *Callao*, and made a good voyage of four years in her to the South Pacific about 1871. Notely shipped in the *Phillip the First*, of Sag Harbor, and we have not heard from him in ten years. Report says that he deserted his ship, reached the Kingsmill group of islands in the Pacific, married the chief's daughter, and is now king there. Robert followed the sea eight years, then took to wrecking, and was drowned in the *Circassian* disaster. As for myself, I shipped at sixteen in the *Pioneer*, of New London, and made my first voyage of seventeen months to Greenland, being frozen in ten months. My next voyage of eighteen months was to the Arctic, in returning from which we were captured and burned by the pirate *Shenandoah*. In 1870 I shipped as mate of the ship *Florida*, of San Francisco, for the Arctic, and next voyage as mate of the *Abbie Bradford*, of New Bedford. We left that port in 1880 for Greenland. Eight months out the captain died of consumption, and I took command of the ship, and after completing the voyage brought the vessel into port."

These brothers, I further learned, became accomplished navigators, with no other education than that afforded by the tribal school. The pretty Congregational chapel Mr. Foster made the basis of some interesting remarks on the moral and religious status of the tribe.

"Some among them have lived and died in the odor of sanctity," he remarked; "but their general spiritual condition is not encouraging, considering the efforts made for their conversion and enlightenment. Love of firewater, as with their fathers, is still their greatest failing. They are not industrious, despising the tilling of the soil, allowing their fine lands here to go to waste, as you see, but no better surfmen or sailors, especially whalemen, can be found. They are wandering and erratic in their habits, usually not more than half the tribe being on the reservation at any one time. Little attention is paid to preserving the purity of the family, negro and white blood being so intermixed that there is not a pure-blood Indian in the tribe."

As before remarked, there are two churches, each with quite a membership, and a school numbering some fifty scholars, the latter being supported by and under the direct control of the State. From the church we drove down to the southern end of the reservation near the sea to a little graveyard, entirely covered with weeds and bushes, where the ten Shinnecocks who perished in the wreck of the *Circassian* were interred, and regained the highway by a series of paths on the west, seeing there several pretty groves with mossy cottages embowered in them — the former often utilized by the young people of Southampton for picnics. The future of the reservation is an interesting question. Its lands are now quite valuable, adjoining plots selling as high as $200 or $300 per acre, and are each year increasing in value. If the Indians could sell, the land would probably long ago have been sold. They, however, only hold it for themselves and their children, the title being vested in the state for the tribe; if partitioned the proceeds would be divided among the Indians, as their individual interests might appear; and so long as a Shinnecock remains it would be difficult for a purchaser to secure a good title.

CHAPTER XXIII

PORT JEFFERSON lies at the head of Setauket Harbor, and, although containing (in 1880) nearly 2000 inhabitants, is so embowered in trees that one coming in from sea would scarcely suspect its existence. Its streets follow primitive cart-paths winding up the hillsides from the hollow in which the business portion of the town lies. Ship-building is the chief, almost the sole industry. As our ship drew up to the dock we heard the clamor of a hundred saws, planes, and hammers, and counted four large brigs on the stocks in process of construction. More than one hundred years ago, we learned, Captain John Wilsie built the first ship here, and the business, although not as good as before the war, is still in a flourishing condition. There are three yards in operation, and a veteran shipwright of eighty told us that he had known ten vessels on the stocks at once. When asked how they could afford to build ships so remote from market, he replied that they put in better material, worked on a

[1] Written in 1887.

better model, and did better work at Port Jefferson
than in other places; hence secured better prices.
"Besides," he continued, "many of the ships built
here are owned by the townspeople. We are thrifty,
build our own ships, furnish the men to man them,
and charter them for cargoes; our vessels are chiefly
engaged in the Southern trade, plying between New
York and Charleston or Savannah." Two steamers,
I learned, besides sailing vessels, were built here one
year, and some eighty yachts are laid up each winter,
their furbishing and refitting in the spring giving
additional animation to the yards. The tourist finds
little to attract in the village aside from its quaintness,
but unless very difficult to please will be charmed by
a sail through its harbor and the waters adjacent.
Setauket Harbor and its tributary, Old Field Bay,
have a common inlet from the Sound and extend west
several miles, forming a labyrinth of straits and bays
lying between wooded points and islands.

To the student of old men and days the whole region
is storied, having been the scene of some of the most
gallant deeds of the whale-boat privateersmen of the
Revolution. It is singular that no more of these men
has been told in history. Many readers are unaware
of their existence; yet they formed an efficient arm of
the Continental service, especially in the transmission
of intelligence, and may be regarded as the germ of
the American navy. Long before Connecticut's war

governor had placed on the Sound the *Spy*, the *Cromwell*, the *Trumbull*, and other audacious privateers to capture the British storeships, the whaleboat crews were abroad, anticipating them in the matter of taking stores, and making reprisals on the Tories who swarmed on the Sound shore of Long Island. The war found them already organized for the capture of the whale and, leaving leviathan, they turned their attention to nobler game. Companies seem to have existed at this time at Stamford, Norwalk, Fairfield, Stratford, Derby, and New Haven, although Fairfield, a leader in the Whig movement, was the center of operations.

Their whale-boats were well adapted to a predatory warfare. They were about thirty-five feet long and were propelled by eight rowers. Each boat carried a large swivel as armament. Their operations were conducted swiftly and silently, usually at night. Sometimes a British fort or magazine on the island was the objective point; sometimes a Tory murder or outrage was to be avenged, or a prominent leader captured in reprisal; again, a supply-ship or armed vessel was the object — two of the latter having been captured and towed into Fairfield during the war. In all cases the leader mustered his men secretly, the boats pushed off at nightfall, rowed swiftly and silently across the Sound, struck their blow, and were out of reach of pursuit when morning broke. Setauket Harbor, directly opposite Fairfield, and but sixteen miles distant, was the landing point of most of these expeditions.

Some of the exploits were not equaled in daring and romance by any feats of the border. In 1777 a large body of the British and Tories had seized the Presbyterian Church at Setauket and converted it into a fortress, using it as a stronghold from which to send out marauding parties. On the 14th of August of that year Colonel Parsons with 150 men embarked at Fairfield in whale-boats, crossed the Sound, and about daybreak made an attack on the fort. The firing had scarcely begun, however, when a messenger came from the boats with the news that several British men-of-war were coming down the Sound, and, fearing that their return might be cut off, the gallant band was forced to retreat.

A second expedition, organized three years later with another object in view, was much more successful. At Mastic, on a point projecting into Great South Bay, the British had erected a formidable fort, encircled by a deep ditch and wall, the whole surrounded by an abattis of sharpened pickets. Several supply vessels and 300 tons of forage were protected by the fort. Hearing through his spies that the fort was garrisoned by but fifty-four men, Colonel Tallmadge determined to capture it, and left Fairfield on the 21st of November, 1780, with eight whale-boats, carrying in all but eighty men. They reached Old Mans — a harbor three miles east of Port Jefferson, at nine o'clock in the evening, and disembarked; but a heavy rain setting in, they were forced to lie all that night and the next day concealed in the bushes. On the second night the rain ceased, and the troops marched across the island — here some twenty miles wide — captured the fort by surprise, dismantled it, burned the vessels, stores, and forage, marched back to their boats with their prisoners, and were in Fairfield by eleven o'clock the next morning, without the loss of a man. Congress passed a resolution highly complimenting the officers and men engaged, and Washington wrote to the commander from Morristown to thank him for his "judicious planning and spirited execution of this business."

A still bolder feat of the whale-boatmen had been executed the year previous. In 1779 the house of General Silliman, in Fairfield, had been surrounded by a body of Tories from Long Island, and the General and his young son were borne away captives. The Americans had no prisoner of equal rank to offer in exchange and decided to procure one. The Hon. Thomas Jones, of Fort Neck, a Justice of the Supreme Court of New York, was selected, and a volunteer company of twenty-five men, commanded by Captain Hawley, set out from Newfield Harbor (now Bridgeport) to capture him. They landed at Stony Brook on the morning of the 4th of November, and began their march to the Judge's residence, more than thirty miles distant, arriving there at 9 o'clock on the evening of the 6th. No man could have been more unsuspicious of danger than he. There was a gay party of young people in the house, and the dance was proceeding merrily, when Captain Hawley and his body of grim retainers appeared at the door. The Judge was found in the hall, and was taken with scant ceremony, a young gentleman named Hewlett being forced to accompany him as a makeweight for the General's son. The party met with many adventures before reaching their boats, being forced to hide in the forest by day, and narrowly escaping capture on two occasions by the light horse, which were soon scouring the country in pursuit. Six laggards were taken, but the others succeeded in regaining their boats, and reached Fairfield on the 8th with their prisoners. It was not, however, until the succeeding May that their exchange was effected.

Quite equal to these in dash and courage were the exploits of Capt. Caleb Brewster, one of the most noted leaders of the service. He was a native of Setauket, but a resident of Fairfield during the war, and accompanied both the expeditions of Colonel Parsons and Major Tallmadge as a volunteer. In 1781 with his whale-boats he boldly attacked a British armed vessel in the Sound, and after a sharp action brought her a prize into Fairfield. Again, on the 7th of December, 1782, from his post at Fairfield he discovered a number of armed boats in the Sound, evidently bent on some predatory excursion, and gave chase. The forces were about equal, and a desperate encounter ensued, nearly every man on both sides being killed or wounded; but the enemy at last escaped with the loss of two of his boats, which were borne into Fairfield in triumph. Brewster himself was shot through the body in this action, but recovered from the wound. The next year, on the 9th of March, 1783, he took the British armed vessel *Fox* in an action lasting but two minutes, and without the loss of a man. In addition to these duties, from the beginning to the end of the struggle he was the confidential agent of Washington in securing information of the enemy's movements.

CHAPTER XXIV

HARVARD'S FIRST GRADUATE

THE REV. NATHANIEL BREWSTER OF SETAUKET

ON a gentle elevation that slopes down to Setauket Harbor on the east, its steeple facing the west, with the village schoolhouse on the right and the Clark Memorial Library on the left, stands the Presbyterian Church of Setauket, a church which has as much history connected with it and of as interesting a character as any of the famous churches of New England. Its early records have been lost, but we know that it was founded in 1660, five years after the Independents of Connecticut had come over and settled Setauket. What is of more general interest is the fact that its first pastor, the Rev. Nathaniel Brewster, a grandson of the famous Elder Brewster of the *Mayflower*, was the first native graduate of Harvard College. Mr. Brewster died during his pastorate here and was buried, according to the present pastor, the Rev. William Littell, who has held his post for thirty years and is a careful student of his church's history, near a corner of the church, though nothing to-day marks the spot. It would be a graceful tribute for the alumni of Har-

vard to erect a simple shaft above his grave in memory
of the first of the long line of able and brilliant men
who have reflected luster on their alma mater.

The second minister, the Rev. George Phillip, also
a graduate of Harvard, was sleeping quietly in the
churchyard which surrounds the sacred edifice, when
the differences of opinion between Britain and her
American colonies culminated in the Revolution.   The
British soon overran Long Island and maintained a
strong garrison here at Setauket, no doubt to overawe
the Independents at New Haven, Fairfield, and other
points on the "Christian shore," as the patriots called
Connecticut.   They seized the Presbyterian church
and turned it into a barracks for their soldiers, as they
did in many other towns of the island, in some cases
using them for stables.

"They built a fort around the church," wrote a
quaint chronicler of the day, "and cast up the bones
of many of the dead.   They destroyed the pulpit and
the whole inside work of the church, and the tombstone of Parson Phillips was among those destroyed.
The minister in charge through all the troublous days
of the Revolution was the Rev. Benjamin Tallmadge,
whose pastorate lasted from 1754 to 1786.   It did not
endear him to the British that his son, Benjamin Tallmadge, Jr., who had settled in Litchfield, Conn., was
one of the boldest, most dashing and most successful
partisan colonels in the Continental service.

In 1797 there came here as pastor the Rev. Zachariah Greene, a man of marked individuality, of whom many good stories are told. When the war broke out, Greene, then a lad of sixteen threw aside his books and entered the patriotic army, doing good service, it is said, in more than one pitched battle; but at last a wound in the shoulder and another in the back disabled him for further military service, and he returned to his books. He was one of Parson's men in the attack on the church at Setauket in 1777, and on assuming the pastorate here made a note of the fact that where formerly he had fought the forces of evil with carnal weapons, he had now come to combat them with spiritual. For fifty years he was acting pastor here, and then for ten years longer pastor emeritus, residing with friends at Hempstead. The older men in the church remember him to this day. Old Father Greene they call him, in speaking of him. He had five fingers on his left hand, and the Presbytery in calling him stipulated that he should keep that hand gloved. He was a good preacher and faithful pastor, the chief founder of the Long Island Bible Society.

During the last years of his pastorate he was assisted by the Rev. John Gile, a young man of much promise. On the very same day that Father Greene started to go to his friends in Hempstead, leaving Mr. Gile in charge of the church, the latter went to Stony Brook Harbor, three miles west, to bring home a sailboat that had been given him. He sailed out of that harbor into the Sound to bring her around into Setauket Bay, and neither man nor boat was ever again heard of.

The present church succeeded in 1812 the one riddled in the Revolution, and is not, therefore, of hoary antiquity.

There are some very old and quaint tombstones in the churchyard. Two very heavy tables of sandstones resting horizontally on piers have a square stone of different color let into the center, on which the inscription is cut. That on the north reads:

" Richard Floyd, Esq., late Colonel of this County and a Judge of the Court of Common Pleas, who deceased February 23, 1737, in ye 73d yr. of his age."

The other stone, without doubt from its position that of his wife, once bore an inscription, but it has been effaced. Why was this done?

CHAPTER XXV

FIRE ISLAND

OFFSPRING of ocean and air, fruitful of nothing but beach grass, hop-toads, snakes, and mosquitoes, Fire Island Beach when I visited it in 1885, still attracted the summer visitor, and held its own bravely with newer and more widely advertised resorts.

A strange bit of earth this beach is, to be sure — a barren, wind-swept, desolate sand-bar, interposed between the Atlantic and the quiet waters of Great South Bay, pushed out nine miles into the ocean, so low and flat that it would seem the first winter storm must blot it out, yet increasing year by year rather than diminishing. It is easy to read its genesis. Ages ago a sand-bar rose out of the waves nine miles off the mainland of Long Island; built up by waves and winds, it grew and lengthened eastward and westward, and in process of time formed a wide smooth beach from Coney Island to Southampton, eighty-one miles, broken at intervals by inlets through which the tides rushed to fill the bays formed by the barrier within. The first glance of the beach shows that man has come over and captured it. Here is the brick

The Surf Hotel, Fire Island
Reproduced from an old print

tower of the lighthouse 185 feet high, the quaint cottage of Life-Saving Station No. 25, and the square signal tower of the Western Union Company. There is also a great hotel,[1] unique in its way, and a model for all seaside hotels, with rows of cottages attached to it, and a mile or more of covered board walks leading to the ocean strand on the south, and to the bayside and steamboat wharf on the north.

As you approach from Babylon across the bay, the hotel looms up like the line of barracks at some great army post, for it is long and low, with three rows of windows like the portholes in a three-decker. The host, Mr. Sammis, is a landlord of the old-fashioned sort, said to be the third oldest inn-keeper on Long Island. After a business career in town as druggist and hotel-keeper, Mr. Sammis came to Fire Island and opened a hotel on the sands. That was in 1855. The first year his hotel was a chowder-house — a sort of day resort for parties from the mainland. It was very successful, and the next year he added 100 feet, and opened the present Surf Hotel. It has grown modestly and safely since then, and is now 625 feet long, with accommodations for 400 guests.

In its old registers may be found the names of some of the best known people of New York and the country. The attractions are mostly such as nature

[1] The Surf Hotel was burned some years ago, and conditions on Fire Island have materially changed since this was written.

offers. A dip in the surf before the eight o'clock
breakfast begins your day. After breakfast you will
find half-a-dozen bronzed bay skippers waiting to
take you to the fishing-grounds. Fine sport has
been had this year in the waters of both bay and
inlet, the gamy bluefish being the special quarry just
now. Trolling is the favorite form of sport with the
guests, but "chumming" is practised. I can see
from my windows now a long line of boats anchored
in the bay, with their lines down in the water, taking
bluefish that have been attracted there by throwing
out bait for days beforehand. The fishermen are
back in time for a plunge in the surf or bay before
dinner. After dinner sailing parties are in order, or
excursions to explore the island — an interesting diver-
sion. The lighthouse and the life-saving station lie
southeast of the hotel, not ten minutes' walk, and
have many visitors.

The old keeper, who has the true nautical flavor
about him, leads the way up the one hundred and
ninety-five steps of the tower to the platform that
runs around the outside just below the huge Fresnel
lens. He is very proud of his light, which is the first
that the great ocean liners sight in approaching
New York from sea, and therefore one of the most
important on the coast. It is a first-order light, with
a lamp of 500-candle power, which pilots have
seen in good weather at a distance of thirty miles,

but whose usual range is twenty-five miles. To feed
the flame of this lamp requires two quarts of the best
kerosene oil every hour. We very much desire to
visit the light after dark, but the keeper is proof against
all blandishments — he points to the regulations of
the Lighthouse Board forbidding visitors to the tower
after sunset, and says the inspector assured him that
it would be as much as his place was worth to disobey
the order. It must be an eerie place up here in a
nor'easter on a winter night, when the tower rocks
under the fury of the gale, and sand, and spray, and
snow clouds the windows. On such nights the keeper
often hears the crash of some heavy objects striking
the glass, and finds next morning beneath his windows
the dead bodies of wild geese and duck which have
struck the tower in the night.

Life-Saving Station No. 25, as before remarked, lies
a little to the southwest, almost within hailing distance.
Its doors have been closed whenever the writer has
passed that way, but a flock of contented chickens gave
evidence that it was inhabited, as is the fact, the keeper
being sole custodian during the summer months, but
with power to summon assistance if it should be required. The Signal Station, or more properly the
reporting station of the Western Union Company,
is the third of the structures which go to make this
barren strip of sand an important commercial center
— although innocent of ships, except those unfortu-

nates whose barnacled ribs may be seen protruding above the sands or swaying in the surf. The Signal Station is a large square tower on the sands, midway between the Surf Hotel and the ocean strand. Fire Island, as before remarked, is the first point of land sighted by the great ocean racers westward bound, and so the Western Union Company maintains here one of its most expert operators, who reports the arrival of steamers not only to their owners, but to those who may have friends on board, several hours before they are due at their docks in New York. The operator is Mr. Peter Keegan, a specialist in his calling and a most interesting man to talk with. If to learn the names of passing ships by reading the signals displayed by them were all he had to do, his work would be mere routine, but to distinguish scores of passing vessels daily by the cut of their jibs or the color of their smoke-stacks, some of them perhaps when only four or five feet of their topmasts are visible, a keenness of vision and wide knowledge of ships and shipping is required. He is a man whose place cannot be filled. Summer and winter since the service was organized in 1878, he has been at his post, with only one day in the year that he can call his own. The room in which he spends most of his time is in the extreme top of the building, and by means of windows and portholes commands a view of the ocean, the inlet, the bay, and the long line of beach. In one corner is a well-selected library, in another the electric key which keeps the vigilant watcher in communication with the outside world, a reclining chair, a cozy rocker, and inviting seats scattered around to complete the furniture. In a third corner is a package of books, tied with a string, that were recovered from the wreck of the *Oregon*, which foundered a few miles off the station. There are two portholes in the southeast corner of the room, and through one a long and powerful telescope is thrust. The little instrument in the corner keeps up a merry clicking — in winter when the hotel is closed, and all the summer visitors departed, the only sound from the outer world that reaches the lonely watcher. "So long as the instrument is in order," says Mr. Keegan, "I don't feel so isolated, for I know that by a few touches I can talk with my most distant friends, or summon aid if needed; but when the cable breaks and the clicking stops, the silence becomes almost unbearable." It is no uncommon thing for the wires to get out of order in the terrible winter storms.

The uninitiated reader no doubt supposes that ships are reported by their signals; if this were the case, the operator's duties would be much simplified, as he would only need to be master of the signal code; but in these days of fierce competition and record-breaking trips, very few of the great ocean-racers run in sufficiently near to display signals — to do so would delay them an hour or more — but keep a straight course

for Sandy Hook Light, thus passing from fifteen to
twenty-five miles out to sea. To the visitor it is a
standing wonder how steamers can be distinguished
and accurately reported at that distance. Mr. Keegan
explains it. "In the first place I know just when to
expect the steamers. The name and hour of sailing
from the other side of each vessel is reported to me,
and I am so familiar with their runs that I know the
very hour that they should pass my station. For
instance, the new French steamer *Bretagne*, one of
four new steamers built for the Havre Line within the
last three years, left Havre on the 20th, and is due here
to-day — the 29th, at this hour — and there are her
topmasts already rising above the horizon. Wednesday I shall look for the fast steamer *City of Paris*,
which left Queenstown at 1.30 P.M. on Thursday, and
will be due here at 8 A.M. on Wednesday. Then,
with my glass, I can see a vessel very distinctly twenty
miles distant, and am enabled to distinguish them by
my special knowledge of their characteristic marks.
Masts and smoke-stacks are the chief distinguishing
features. I have reported vessels when but four or
five feet of their masts were visible."

"Do you never make mistakes?" is asked.

"But one in four years," he replied, "and this is how
it happened: I was expecting a certain steamer, a slow
boat, due to pass some time in the night. Steamers
passing at night display no signals by which I can tell

their names, but simply burn a signal indicating the line to which they belong. At midnight a steamer passed and showed the signal of the line to which the expected boat belonged, and I naturally inferred it was she, and so reported, but as it turned out the company had sent a second boat immediately after the first, and she was the one that displayed the signal."

"Are mistakes attended with serious results?"

"They would cause great confusion and expense," is the reply. "For instance, *La Bretagne*, which you see just coming into view out there, and which I have just reported, has, say, 300 cabin passengers on board That means that 200 messages announcing her arrival are now being sent out to friends of persons on board, and of course if the wrong vessel is reported, no end of annoyance and loss would be caused."

"You must have had some thrilling and exciting experiences while keeping your lonely vigils."

"In the matter of shipwrecks and loss of life," he replied, "yes; I suppose I saw the last signal of the gallant fellows on the pilot boat *Columbia*, which disappeared so mysteriously off Fire Island one dark night, leaving not a trace. That night I sighted the *Alaska* and reported her; a few minutes later I saw a pilot boat setting her signal; then suddenly the latter's lights went out, and I saw the steamer lying to and cruising about as if searching for something. She did not leave until daylight, and reported being in collision with some vessel. The most singular part of it was that not a trace of the *Columbia* or of her crew was ever discovered. That famous disaster, the sinking of the *Oregon*, was first reported by me. It was the morning of March 14, 1887 — Sunday; I had scheduled her to pass about sunrise, and at 5.30, sweeping the horizon with my glass, I saw a trail of smoke rising above the sea. 'It is the *Oregon* coming up,' I said, and waited for her to come nearer. As her smoke-stacks came into view I saw that something was wrong, but what, I could not make out, as she showed no signals of distress. At once I sent the main office this telegram:

"'Steamer *Oregon*, southeast bound in, apparently in trouble.   KEEGAN.'

"An hour later she changed her course and headed for the beach, flying the British ensign union down at masthead — a signal showing great extremity, and I knew she needed assistance at once. Looking about for some one to go to her aid, I saw pilot boat No. 11 and the schooner *Fanny Gorham* in the offing and signaled both. The sea was quite smooth, and both at once headed for the disabled *Oregon*. All were so far down the horizon that I could not see the boats which transferred the steamer's passengers to the schooner, but all were got safely on board. The *Oregon* kept dropping below the sea line all the morning, but whether she was sinking or only drifting I could not tell. Later I saw the steamer *Fulda* come up and take off the rescued passengers from the schooner. As she passed me she signaled, '*Oregon* sunk; passengers all saved and on board,' which I at once reported to the office at New York — the first announcement of the disaster given the public. Pilot boat No. 11 — the *Phantom* — foundered at sea in the blizzard just a year later, and all on board were lost. I also sent her owners the first news of the stranding of the *Scotia*, which struck on a shelving bar fifteen miles east of here while nearly at full speed. I first saw her headed for the beach about five o'clock in the morning, with both masts gone. Later I made out her name from her signal flag, which was suspended from between her smoke-stacks, and at once reported her plight to her owners, who sent tugs of the Merritt Wrecking Company to pull her off."

"The *Hilton Castle* foundered off here, did she not?"

"Yes. I saw her the night before, but being only a freight boat I paid no attention to her. She went down during the night. I saw our life-saving crew go out next morning through the surf and bring in one of her boats with eight men in it, and a little later saw a schooner pick up the other boat. These facts I also reported."

Sometimes the operator's duties are of a more grisly character, as when he jots down and flashes over the wires descriptions of dead bodies thrown upon the beach by the sea. The other Sunday Capt. John Wicks of the Life-Saving Station came in and reported finding the body of a man on the beach about a mile east of the station, clad in only a shirt and trousers, which had been in the water some eight days. "A clerk, evidently," said the operator, "for he had in his pockets two elastic bands and an eraser such as are used in offices — a well-dressed man, stout, with features unrecognizable. We cannot tell where he came from, unless from a passing ship — not from New York, certainly, for the prevailing winds of late have been from eastward. There was nothing else in his pockets except part of a copy of the New York *World* of July 20. We at first thought the body might be that of Hogan, the missing aeronaut, but as the latter made his ascent on the 16th, the paper of the 20th proved that it was not he."

INDEX

INDEX